Spiritual Moms is also a man's book. Wise and practical, I gained much from it.

—*Dick Schneider,*
Senior Staff Editor of Guideposts

Lynn Scarborough tackles the theme of spiritual motherhood with her characteristic passion and energetic optimism. The personal stories make the book real and relevant. This is not the domain of the few; this is for you!

—*Bob Sorge,*
author of Envy: The Enemy Within

As a grandmother and getting close to retirement, I have sometimes thought that it would soon be time to step back from things. After reading Lynn's inspirational guide, I find I have so many things I now want to do. I feel I can and want to continue to be a woman of influence.

—*Winnie Bartel,*
Chairman of the Women's Commission
for World Evangelical Alliance

Many people still assume women live blissful lives caring for husbands and children with little reason to be involved in the lives of others. Like kicking off high heels after a weeklong convention, or breaking into a loaf of warm bread, Lynn Scarborough's book gives sweet relief to real life and fills the spiritual senses with biblical destiny. *Spiritual Moms* satisfies.

—*Joann Cole Webster,*
author and publisher

If you want to be used of God to influence women for Him, *Spiritual Moms* should be on your reading list. Scarborough's examples and insights will motivate you to become a spiritual mom to others for God's kingdom and glory.

—*Cheryl Reccord,*
author and speaker

Spiritual Moms is a powerful and timely book that encourages and strengthens women. Don't be misled by the title—both men and women will enjoy this book that brings generations together.

—*Olen Griffing,*
pastor, Antioch Oasis International

Reading this book will prepare your heart to better equip other men and women to walk in their intended God-given role.

—*Dr. Cornell Haan,*
National Facilitator of Ministry Networks, Mission America

Spiritual Moms

AN INSPIRATIONAL GUIDE
FOR WOMEN OF INFLUENCE

Lynn Wilford Scarborough

new
hope
PUBLISHERS

Birmingham, Alabama

New Hope® Publishers
P. O. Box 12065
Birmingham, AL 35202-2065
www.newhopepubl.com

Library of Congress Cataloging-in-Publication Data
Scarborough, Lynn Wilford.
Spiritual moms : an inspiration guide for women of influence / by
Lynn Wilford Scarborough.
p. cm.
ISBN 1-56309-824-5 (pbk.)
1. Mothers-Religious life. 2. Spiritual life-Christianity. I.
Title.
BV4529.18.S32 2004
248.8'431—dc22
2003026723

ISBN: 1-56309-824-5
N044112 • 0404 • 7.5M1

Dedication

To my sweet Lord—
May the sight of Your face be my daily grace.

To my mom and all the women in my family—
I cherish your sacrifices, embrace your joy, and celebrate your talents.

To all the spiritual moms in my life—
I honor your wisdom, bless your faith, and thank you for your love.

To spiritual moms of the present—
I rejoice in your testimony, respect your courage, and embrace your fellowship.

Blessed is she who believed —Luke 1:45

This book is dedicated to spiritual moms everywhere, every time, everyplace.

Spiritual moms who have:
  Seen beyond light
  Reached beyond convenience
  Cared beyond self
  Pushed beyond pain
  Endured beyond vision
  Prayed beyond hope
  Loved beyond measure

Table of Contents

Section Three: You Can Be a Spiritual Mom

Section Four: Spiritual Mothers in the Bible

Calling All Spiritual Moms

The hand that rocks the cradle
will change the world,
The heart that trains the soul
will reach the nations,
But the spirit that awakens
the destiny of another,
transforms the universe.

I was a lonely college student when I arrived at the University of Texas. I had left my home in the Washington, D.C., area, my family, a strong church with an active youth group, and dozens of Christian friends to attend school in the foreign land of the West. I was homesick and in culture shock. One day I decided to go to the Episcopal church that was closest to my dorm in Austin, the historic St. David's, to see if I could find some new friends.

I was disappointed to find that they didn't have an active college group or prayer outreach. "But if you are interested in prayer," said the rector, "you should talk to Louise, who leads a prayer group during the week. In fact, I think that she may be upstairs in the sanctuary now. Why don't you go up and say hi?" So I went in search of Louise, not because I was interested but simply to be courteous to the pastor. When I came to the huge, 12-foot walnut doors that led into the sanctuary, I was a little intimidated. I considered leaving and catching the bus back to the dorm in time for dinner. Instead, something prompted me to pull the heavy door open and walk into the sanctuary. I intended only to say a quick hello to this "prayer woman," but instead I stepped into a remarkable relationship with one of my first spiritual moms.

The first time I saw Louise walking toward me down the aisle of the empty church, she seemed to glow. I don't know if it was the radiant sparkle in her eyes or the way the light from the late afternoon sun stretched through the antique stained-glass windows that captured my attention. This woman, whom others talked about in semi-hushed tones, seemed to have light coming from inside her. Rainbow puddles of light kissed her shoulders as she came toward me. Her eyes were joyful, and her warm smile made me relax and smile back. She gave me the loving look of a grandmother with a secret.

Louise wanted to know all about me and my love for the Lord. Over the next four years, as I finished my undergraduate and MFA degrees, she was always there to listen, pray, counsel, and encourage. And during the following five, ten, and twenty years, this wonderful saint has been there for me to help shine the light of God into every joy and sorrow in my life, and to wash with prayer every experience, challenge, and celebration.

As a theater major I tended to be creative and very spontaneous in my spiritual expression and was always writing, singing, miming, or performing. Louise was a kind and generous audience, with a quick laugh, who always gave a non-judgmental comment, such as, "That's nice, dear, but do you really think that the disciples would have said that?" She loved to have me come over and sing the songs that I wrote or learned at the college worship group. Louise always wanted to know what Scriptures and books I was reading, would listen to me recite my Scripture memory verse, or would have me explain the Sunday school lesson I was writing. When I spent a challenging year in seminary, she patiently prayed for me and encouraged me to pursue God.

All during my college days and ever since, Louise has been ready with an ear, word, and prayer for me. Time after time, I have called her and she has had exactly the right Scripture that answers a question or gave me the solution to a problem. Even if we had not talked in a while, whenever I called she would have just read a Scripture passage that was exactly what I needed to hear. When it came to my life and spiritual walk, Louise had a direct phone line to God's throne room. In fact, when I go through my journals from college, it always makes me smile to find an entry that begins, "Called Louise and she said that the Lord..."

Louise's faith is so real, so joyful, so deep, and so passionate that it made me dive deeper into the waters of faith. Her life was a model and example that Paul spoke of: "These things that I do, do also..."

Louise taught and re-taught me that everything—every problem, every challenge, every disappointment, every hope, and every vision—has to be brought to the throne of grace. She taught me that God's plans are more important than our own, and the sooner we really turn our lives and schedules over to His guidance, the better off we will be. Even to this day, more than twenty years since our friendship began, Louise still teaches me whenever we speak. Louise loves the Lord and always wants to learn more about Jesus.

She doesn't get out much now to participate in the bi-weekly prayer meetings she started and ran for thirty years. Louise's knees are swollen and inflexible from thousands of hours spent on them. A widow whose only child died years ago, she needs round-the-clock assistance to live. Yet her phone still rings all day with people calling for prayer, counsel, and with best wishes. As a spiritual mom, Louise will never retire, and for that I am so thankful.

I have been fortunate to have Louise and so many other wonderful women of God in my life. I have been richly blessed with spiritual moms who have poured their lives into me with abandon. This book is a tribute to them and the thousands upon thousands of other spiritual mothers who fill our churches and serve the body of Christ tirelessly.

God's "Power Team"

From the very beginning, God created the family to help lead the children and future generations to the faith. A child needs food, love, and training to mature into an adult, and the Christian needs spiritual food, love, and training to mature as well. From baptism to the commissioning ceremony, a Christian requires a tremendous amount of teaching, training, love, and direction to produce healthy, productive, and balanced Christians.

Children require both nurture and discipline to help them grow. Raising spiritual children requires the same skills, except it may be more difficult to recognize the needs because the packages are different. It's easy to know when to get a Band-Aid for a four-year-old, but it's sometimes hard to tell when that forty-five-year-old "Christian newborn" needs a hug and word of encouragement.

Spiritual mothers and fathers are co-laborers in the soul vineyard. God woos the spirit, Christ enters the heart, and the Spirit renews the soul, yet the incredible privilege of parenting and raising God's children is given to both men and women.

It takes the influence of a dad and mom to raise a child; likewise, it takes spiritual dads and moms, working together with God, to develop healthy men and women of faith. There are many books that train men to be spiritual fathers; however, it is important to recognize and affirm the equally important roles that spiritual mothers have in building the Kingdom.

Spiritual Moms Are Everywhere!

Spiritual moms or mothers are not a new concept, but only a new term. Spiritual moms have been functioning in the faith since Old Testament times. Today, women are in ministry from the jungles of Brazil to the White House. A spiritual mother can be a mom, professional woman, secretary, teacher, Bible study leader, pastor's wife, or prayer leader. The job they have is not important; what *is* important is who and what they are to those around them. If the father is the head of the home, then the mother is the heart. The spiritual mother can function to help share the heart of God with others in the community, neighborhood, school, church, workplace, or cell group. All that a natural mother is to a family, a spiritual mother is to the children of God in her life.

If you look around, you will be amazed at how much spiritual moms do. If you think back in your life, you might discover that there were spiritual moms who helped you along the spiritual path. You may even find that you have been a spiritual mom to others.

Spiritual mothers have not been the subject of many books and sermons, but it doesn't mean that they don't exist. Sarah, Rachel, Naomi, Deborah, Elizabeth, Esther, Anna, Mary, and Lydia were all spiritual mothers to those around them. Hilda of Whitby, Florence Nightingale, Lucretia Mott, Harriet Tubman, Corrie Ten Boom, Mother Teresa, and Catherine Marshall were spiritual mothers in more modern history.

The truth is that spiritual mothers *have always been* and *will always be* integral to the work of the gospel. We often don't remember how important something is because it is so familiar. Spiritual mothers have a vital God-given role in ministry, and their contributions are critical to the growth and future of the church.

Honor the Obvious

Before the terrorist attacks of September 11, 2001, most people took police officers and firefighters for granted. Now they are appreciated and loved for the sacrifices they make. Did police officers and firefighters risk their lives before 9/11? Yes, and they still do, everyday. Were they any less courageous or honorable after this date? No, they always were and will be, in hundreds of cities, a thousand times a year. What changed was the level of awareness and appreciation that the general public had for them.

The Scriptures tell us to honor our father and our mother so that it may be well with us and that our days may be increased. As we honor our physical fathers and mothers, we should do the same for the spiritual fathers and mothers. This means more than a corsage on Mother's Day and Christmas. It means both personally and publicly appreciating and celebrating the gifts, sacrifices, and contributions of spiritual fathers and mothers. By acknowledging and honoring the godly men and women in our lives, it encourages and challenges other men and women to grow and participate in the same manner for the glory of God.

Help the Orphans

There are spiritual orphans everywhere. I know because I was one. Fortunately, the Lord generously provided many spiritual mothers and fathers who have poured truth, Scripture, and love into my life. Children learn by imitating their parents, their peers, and the adults around them. Paul tells his many spiritual children to imitate him in actions, attitudes, and spiritual gifts. I have been fortunate to have many incredible spiritual mothers to imitate. Now, in turn, I am a spiritual mom and sharing the wealth of wisdom and understanding that they generously added to my life.

All Hands and Hearts on Deck

In times of war, everyone joins in the war effort, both at the battlefront and at home. In times of peace, the role of the soldier takes on the "professional" status, maintaining peace and performing other delegated duties. In a spiritual sense, our world is at war. The "professionals only need apply" period is behind us; our nations, neighborhoods, and families are in crisis, and all hands and hearts are needed to "man and woman" the battle stations. In the spiritual realm, this means that from the pulpit to the classroom, from the boardroom to the grocery store, we all need to take part in the Great Commission. It's a big job, and God wants you!

Salvation is only the first step into the Kingdom. Accepting the Lord is like the first breath and cry of a newborn. The work really begins after that. If we are to bring in the harvest and raise men and women of faith who stand the test and are able to overcome the world, then we need more spiritual fathers and mothers. The harvest is waiting and the fields are ripe. We need everyone to help bring in the harvest of souls. The gifts, talents, and energies of every man, woman, youth, and child are needed to build the body of Christ, equip the saints, and prepare this world for the kingdom that is coming.

Spiritual Mom: Job Description

What do spiritual moms do? They love, guide, mentor, train, and encourage those who are placed in their lives. In my case, they prayed for me, listened to me, cooked for me, taught me, and cried with me.

They cleaned me up when shame nearly buried me. They touched my life with truth. They freed me from the prison of guilt and confusion. They turned on the light when darkness filled my mind. They encouraged me when I was tired and picked me up when I fell. But most of all, they simply loved me and, in doing so, demonstrated the love of God.

What will you gain from this book?

- Through Scripture, history, stories, and testimonies of spiritual moms, you will be inspired and challenged.
- If you need a spiritual mom, I hope that this book will help you find one.
- If you are a spiritual mom, I hope you will be encouraged and inspired.
- If you have a spiritual mom or several, this book will help you thank them.
- If you feel you are called to be a spiritual mom, this book will help teach you through Scriptures, stories, and the life examples of other great women.
- If you are in ministry, I hope that you will recognize and appreciate the spiritual moms who support you, give to you, and pray for you.
- If you are a pastor, I hope that you will empower and encourage the spiritual moms around you to even greater fruitfulness and godly service.

- If you care about saving souls and making life-long followers of Jesus Christ, this book will give you ways to recruit, train, and increase a remarkable army to the glory of the Father.

As with any important work, the payoff may not be immediate, but the results will stand for eternity!

How to Be a Spiritual Mom

Chapter One

How to Spot a Spiritual Mom!

From casserole queen to congressperson
From Sunday School guru to Kool-Aid mom,
From prayer momma to producer diva,
Spiritual moms are building God's family
One heart and one soul at a time.

One of my friends, Rachael, is the stay-at-home mom for her neighborhood. Rachael always tells people that the reason she doesn't have a career is that she always wanted to be the "Kool-Aid mom" in the neighborhood. And unlike a majority of their friends, Rachael and her husband made the decision and financial commitment that Rachael's first priority would be the family, her husband, and their son, Adam. But Rachael wasn't only a mother to her own son. Because of her availability to them, she was able to help, comfort, and influence many children in her neighborhood. She is a spiritual mom.

She knows that the challenges families face in today's world are much more complex and messy than we like to accept. The challenges of today's economic pressures, the divorce rate, blended families, drugs, and sexual pressures have created generations of wounded people.

Rachael and her husband made sure that their house was one where Adam and his teenage friends could hang out. Rachael always said that even though it was challenging to be the "Grand Central Station" of the neighborhood, it was worth it to be able to know what was going on in her son's life. That way she could have an influence and be there when her son and his many friends needed to talk. And talk they did! In talking with them, Rachael was able to love, affirm, encourage, bless, correct, and find out about issues in the teen world before they became problems.

The Kool-Aid mom often came to the rescue. Being a safe person for teens to talk with allowed her to help them deal with issues such as sex, drugs, rebellion, abuse, and peer pressure. When she discovered the kids were not being truthful about what they were doing and whose house they were staying at, the Kool-Aid mom called for a potluck supper to help form a neighborhood parents' coalition. The potluck supper improved the lines of communication among the parents, and the teens eventually had better boundaries.

The influence Rachael has had upon the teens who have flowed through her house is amazing and impossible to fully measure. To date, several of Rachael's young people and their family members have become Christians and are now going to church. There have been renewed commitments to honesty, moral integrity, and purity. One of the biggest challenges children and youth face today is knowing the difference between right and wrong. By being a listening ear and loving voice, Rachael has been able to not only influence her son, but also his friends, their families, and the entire neighborhood for the Lord.

The Growth of a Soul

It takes time for a person to grow into adulthood and spiritual maturity. There are a lot of meals between the first bottle of spiritual milk to the solid meat of truth. There are lessons to be learned and trials to be faced. From the bassinet to college graduation, it takes both a mother and a father to raise a healthy child.

In our society of "fatherless children," the focus has been on the need for a father figure in a child's life. But when you evaluate the number of working moms and the amount of time that children actually spend with their parents, it seems that in truth, we have a "parentless generation." The suffering created by this erosion of the family has severely impacted our society.

America is blessed to have some of the most dedicated, broad-reaching, and creative ministry efforts on earth. Churches are everywhere, Bibles are available in supermarkets, and the airwaves are filled with hundreds of hours of great Christian programming. We are able to buy the best works of talented Christian musicians and writers. However, when you look at how much money Americans spend on evangelism, events, Bibles, and Christian radio and television, and compare those numbers to church growth statistics, pitiful tithing rates, and the lack of long-term growth, it is obvious that evangelism efforts are not producing results equal to the amount of effort exerted. There must be a better way to reach, teach, and retain church members.

In this age of speedy communication, people still need the most important thing of all: human love and the love of God. Love cannot be transmitted through the computer screen or through CD players. Love comes from the time we spend with others. And just as it takes a lot of time, energy, and love to raise healthy kids, the same is true with our spiritual children. My Sunday school kids, who are much more tech-savvy than I am, still respond best to love. The kids come streaming into class and literally stand in line for their weekly hug. In church you will see them making a beeline for a favorite adult to get that hug or word of encouragement or to show them the war scars from their in-line skates. The buzzword for today's youth is "extreme." With the speed that the world is going, we need extreme effort by both spiritual mothers and fathers to reach this world and this generation.

Characteristics of a Spiritual Mom

Spiritual moms are one of God's best solutions to touch lives. Even people who have terrific relationships with their biological moms can find their lives enriched by the investment of a spiritual mom in their lives. A spiritual mom is a person who nurtures and cares for a growing Christian. That's it. A spiritual mom provides loving guidance in someone's spiritual life, offering wisdom, spiritual food, perspective on life, and a strong sense of belong to Christian family. The relationship can be long- or short-term, long-distance or in close proximity. The people involved may never call it "spiritual mothering." But they know it makes a crucial difference in their spiritual life. You probably know several spiritual moms but don't realize it. Here are some of the ways to spot a spiritual mom.

Look for the flowers. Spiritual mothers flourish where planted, and the amazing result is that others around them bloom also. Just like plants around a water faucet, they are a little taller, a little stronger and healthier because of their close proximity to the water. Those who live or work near a spiritual mom will tend to thrive around the "Living Water" that flows from her.

Look for the fruit that refreshes. Have you ever been around someone who renews your heart and spirit? Spiritual moms have this amazing ability to make you feel renewed when you're around them. Their homes remind me of my grandparents' home in the mountains—a place to take a long nap and not feel guilty about it. When you leave a spiritual mom, whether it's after a thirty-minute chat or a three-day visit, you leave feeling strengthened and ready to face the world. Spiritual moms give your spirit a vacation from the "yuck" of the world. Spiritual moms help take the weight of guilt and sin off your back. They can do this because they help to plug you into the real Source of strength and peace.

Open-heart policy. Another way to spot a spiritual mom is that you will find yourself talking to her about your deepest concerns, thoughts, fears, dreams, and the prayers of your heart. Spiritual moms have a way of making you feel so safe and comfortable that you immediately want to tell them everything. When I visit one of my spiritual moms, we are often awake—talking, laughing, and crying—long after everyone has gone to bed.

Check your sin at the door. Spiritual moms also have the ability to make you evaluate yourself quickly. Just like a sailor who remembers not to swear in front of his grandmother, spiritual moms help turn up the heat on our consciences. Just as the threat "I'm gonna tell mom" is often enough to cause children to be obedient, the presence of a spiritual mom has a way of making us do a quick check on our actions, thoughts, and attitudes.

The mom sense of knowing. Moms have a way of knowing what is wrong before you even say something. In nature the body of a breast-feeding mother will produce antibodies for her child automatically, even if she hasn't been exposed to that particular germ. Just as the mother's physical body knows what the child needs, a spiritual mom will know what you need spiritually. When you speak to her she may have a story, Scripture, song, tape, or sermon waiting for you. Often when I call Louise, one of my spiritual mothers, she tells me she has been praying for me and reads me a Scripture that is perfect for the need at hand.

Spiritual X-ray vision. Along the same lines, spiritual moms have a way of being able to quickly pinpoint the challenge, sin, problem, or hurt you are facing. It's as if they have X-ray vision to identify the root problem, even if it's hidden beneath layers of denial. During graduate school, Anne, one of my spiritual moms, asked me what was wrong with me. I was shocked. We had been laughing and joking and I didn't feel like anything was wrong. She insisted, and said that she thought I was hurt about something and that I was acting like a clown to cover it up. I hadn't a clue as to what she was talking about. Three days later it hit me like a ton of bricks as anger, pain, and frustration bubbled up inside me. I had been hurt by judgmental attitudes that some people in my fellowship group had expressed toward me. It had taken these emotions three days to come to the surface. My spiritual mom had sensed my wound and had the courage to confront me with it. She let me stew in my denial until finally I had the emotional stamina to recognize, deal with, and respond to the situation.

Within churches, ministries, or companies, spiritual mothers will often see and know things before the leadership or congregation figure it out. It's a wise leader who learns to take the spiritual mother into his/her counsel to hear what the Lord has been saying to her and how the Spirit has been leading her to pray.

Lots of fresh-baked bread. Don't you love the smell of fresh bread? Who can resist having a piece straight from the oven with butter and milk? When we think of spiritual mothers, we are reminded that they know how to serve up the Word. No matter the form—milk, fruit, or meat—spiritual mothers have a way of feeding you with the Word of God without you even knowing, or rather, without you objecting to it. Spiritual mothers love to feed people in the Spirit. They may not be great chefs in the kitchen, but a spiritual mother knows how to set a banquet table of revelation before you.

Hugs, hugs, and more hugs. This is one of the best things about mothers—hugs. I believe that a hug is a touch from God in human form. We all know about sickly babies who die because of the lack of a loving touch. We also know that these same babies, if touched and held frequently, often overcome the odds. I wonder how many baby Christians have been lost because no one was there to touch and love them? How much spiritual potential has shriveled on the vine when all that was needed was a human relationship to keep them going? There are a lot of hug-deprived people in this world. Who knows what would happen if we would simply start hugging more people each day?

True reflection. Spiritual mothers give you a true reflection of yourself and challenge you with it even though you may not see your gifts or potential at all. Spiritual mothers have a way of seeing into the future and calling for the hope and destiny that God has planned for your life. When you are in the valley, spiritual mothers come down from the mountain and hold your hand while you walk through it.

Never too old to be a cheerleader. One of the most important things spiritual mothers have done for me is to be the encouraging voices in the dark. Kids fall down a lot, and it's the moms who pick them up, hug them, bind the wound, dry the tears, and send them out the door to get on the bike again. The same is true with the spiritual walk, especially the older you are. In order to grow and change, children—both spiritual and natural—need a lot of support, hugs, and love. Spiritual mothers are critically important in providing the love and helping hand needed by baby Christians.

Heroes of the Heart

Above all else, guard your heart, for it is the wellspring of life.
—Proverbs 4:23 NIV

Keep your heart with all diligence, for out of it spring the issues of life.
—Proverbs 4:23 NKJV

The heart is the wellspring and source of life for every person, home, leader, king, and country. The heart is the axis around which our life rotates. It guides us, strengthens us, enlightens us, and prepares us.

The heart is the largest and strongest muscle mass in the body. It is the first organ that grows in the fetus, even before the brain. The heart is the first and most important organ that contributes to all growth, nourishment, health, healing, and function. The heart can think, too. Recent scientific studies from cardiologists have revealed that the heart creates neurological impulses, which means that the heart has memories and can "think." There are dozens of stories about heart transplant patients who have experienced the memories and emotions of the heart donor.

As any person in love will tell you, the leading of the heart is far stronger than that of the head. People are most happy when they are in love, following their heart and pursuing their passion. A broken heart leads to despair; a mended heart rejoices. Out of the abundance of the heart a person speaks. The heart of a lover is a rich garden.

A person must accept Christ into his or her heart, not head, to be saved. God even gives us a new heart when we seek Him. "*I will give you a new heart and put a new spirit within you; I will take the heart of stone out of your flesh and give you a heart of flesh*" (Ezekiel 36:26 NKJV).

Just as the mother is the heart of a home, a spiritual

mother helps to train the heart of a person's spirit. Our western culture has been dominated by the brain, logic, knowledge, and intellect. Just as too much head knowledge can be a major block to faith, too much intellectual Christianity can be a block to the fullness of the Christian life.

What the World Needs Now

"Too much religion and not enough love" was the complaint about the church a friend of mine visited. Jesus said that the world would know us by our love, not our knowledge. It is love that helps us reach the lost. It is love that is the most compelling gift we have. So, as Paul admonished, "Let our love abound," and may our hearts be enlarged.

Do you remember the song from the '70s, "What the World Needs Now Is Love"? What the *church* needs now is more love. What the world needs is the love of Christ.

We need more love and we need more loving hearts.

We need more love in our homes, relationships, churches, workplaces, everywhere.

Love is the water of life and the healer of dry spirits. Love flows from the heart of God. Love makes things grow, especially in the spirit. Love is the living water that helps people grow and bear lots of spiritual fruit. Spiritual moms provide a fountain of love from the river of God.

Nancy Huston Hansen:
Delivery Room with a Worldview

Faith-based foundations provide the critical support that gives life to many ministries and kingdom projects. Nancy

Huston Hansen, of the Huston Foundation, is a spiritual mother who has helped develop, guide, and support hundreds of ministries for more than 30 years. Nancy has directed funds from the Huston Foundation to a wide range of projects, among them inner-city medical clinics, citywide ministry outreaches, literacy and prayer initiatives, compassion services such as Mercy MedFlight, video projects such as *Transformations* and *Somebody Cares*, women's initiatives, and evangelical outreaches. Very few people ever have the opportunity to control as much money as Nancy does. She finds great satisfaction in seeing that Huston Foundation money is given to projects that accomplish God's purposes in the world. Nancy shares:

Most people have very little understanding of what foundations do. My job is multi-faceted—it's almost like being a birth coach. We do more than simply giving people a check; it is helping people in ministry become what God has called them to be. Foundations often provide structure and counsel, warning burgeoning ministries of potential problems. Sometimes they are there to network with others who can add strength and dimension to the ministry's vision.

Before I get involved with funding a ministry, I ask, "Is it a God thing?" and then I pray about what part I am to take in it. Our foundation provides "seed grants," which are like startup grants. A seed grant is given to a fledgling organization that many other foundations won't fund. I will work with them and get other people or funders involved.

We like to choose unique projects, things that are not being done yet. We make sure it is providing a service to the community, it is innovative, and it fills a niche. We usually continue funding the ministry until other major funders come in. Then we move on to another one. We like to plant, see growth, and then move on.

It takes a spiritual mother to get a program up and going. God has taken me through many adventures. One of the biggest challenges is discerning what is really God-centered. One man came to us for funding for a program for kids dying of cancer. Something didn't seem right. When I asked him what they do, he said they have parties for kids at hospital wards and give out balloons and treats. It turned out they were doing little entertainments for these dying children, then using the opportunity to raise more donations from grieving parents. There was no spiritual value at all, just horrible manipulation. Naturally, we didn't fund them.

When we find a truly dedicated ministry, we know they usually go through unbelievable testing. Unless a seed goes into the ground and dies, it won't bear fruit. As a funder, you have to go through the death process with them, and stay with them even when it looks like they aren't going to make it, because you know it is a God-given work.

Best Pick-Up Lines for Spiritual Moms

1. Hello, how are you?

2. Did you need some help?

3. What's your name?

4. You are so special.

5. I'd like to get to know you.

6. Can I hold your baby, bag, or Bible?

7. Where did you get that outfit?

8. I know that God really wants to use you.

9. Want to have lunch, dinner, a latte, or a Slim-Fast?

10. So glad you came.

11. Where's your favorite discount store?

12. How can I pray for you?

Chapter Two

A Far-Reaching Influence

Some events sweep into one's memory like a rain-swollen river. After the flood of experiences has passed, one awakens to find the shores of your understanding changed forever. It was the evening of September 2, 2000, the date of an event called The Call, DC. For an unforgettable twelve hours, almost half a million young people and their parents gathered together on the Mall at the base of the Capitol building to pray, fast, worship, and intercede for our nation. From the platform dozens of spiritual fathers and mothers challenged and commissioned the "Gen-Nexters" to reach the world with the gospel.

The sights and sounds were remarkable, as only the passion of youth can command—energetic prayer, hip-hop worship teams, unbridled weeping, solemn foot washing, shouts of praise, joyous dancing, rainbow-hued hair, multicultural smiles, and countless healing embraces. Even during the late summer downpour, thousands remained, ignoring their rain-drenched t-shirts. New friends huddled under cardboard umbrellas while others reached toward heaven's free baptism.

Watching from the video production truck next to the director, I had the best seat in the house. From a dozen different angles, I watched emotions on thousands of passionate faces change from celebration to repentance to joy and hunger for God's presence. The images on a dozen television screens provided a moment of understanding of how the multi-eyed cherubim must feel as they look upon the beauty of the Lord.

As I watched, I tried to memorize everything that I saw, but there was more than anyone could humanly absorb. Throughout the day, the crew in the truck was often frozen in position. We were mesmerized. We watched wave upon wave of celebration and spiritual passion wash over the crowd. The crowd was so large that there were Jumbotrons two miles back from the stage. When cameras would take a shot from the back of the crowd, we could see that the youth in the back were as intent as the crowd at the front.

In the production truck and over the headset I would hear the crew continually exclaiming, "Awesome! Look at that! How incredible!" The entire production team was overwhelmed to see the commitment and passion that the younger generations demonstrated for the Lord. We were so busy we were unable to do what we felt like doing—dissolving in tears of joy and conviction.

It had been one of those days when history had been made, and hopefully the future had been shaped. I walked back to the hotel exhausted, yet the buzz of joy would guarantee that we'd be up talking into the early morning hours. It was one of those intoxicating times when the intense emotions make you feel like you are floating, yet every detail is memorable. The twilight mist seemed to glow with love in a floating haze of glory.

Conversation at The Call, DC

Walking into the hotel lobby, I noticed that Dr. Bill Bright was waiting to go out to dinner. I greeted him and we shared impressions and celebrated the day. In our conversation I mentioned that I had been researching spiritual mothers. He asked me if I had seen a recent book, *100 Christian Women Who Changed the 20th Century,* by Helen Kooiman Hosier. I replied that I had, and he said, "You know, the three people that most influenced my life are in that book: my mother, my wife, and Henrietta Mears."

How incredible to hear that this remarkable Christian leader, founder of the Campus Crusade organization, which has reached millions for the gospel, was most influenced by three dynamic spiritual mothers. Then a few minutes later, Vonette Bright walked up with her famous smile and gracious manner and affirmed Dr. Bright's comment. What a wonderful testimony to the importance of spiritual mothers! The ministry of Dr. Bill Bright has enriched many and been an invaluable contribution to my own spiritual walk. And that means that these three remarkable women who influenced Dr. Bright have also influenced and blessed me. They share in my successes and spiritual fruit.

As the Brights walked out of the hotel for their dinner appointment, I was further committed to discovering more about spiritual moms and how to become one. I wanted to help Christians understand how important spiritual mothers have been in the history of the church and will be to the future.

Henrietta Mears—A Legacy of Leaders

I had heard the name of Henrietta Mears for years and had even bought a copy of her biography when I was a teenager, but I didn't realize how remarkable the scope of her ministry was until a conversation over dinner.

It was February 2000 in Washington, D.C., and I was spending the weekend with my friend, Debbie, and her mother, Doris. The ice and snow made us opt to stay in for dinner. As we cooked, I began to ask Doris questions about how she and her husband met and got involved in ministry.

Doris began to tell me how, when she lived in Los Angeles in her twenties, she heard about this great Bible study at First Presbyterian Church in Hollywood. A woman led it. It was quite a drive for Doris, but she loaded up the car with a couple of girlfriends and headed out. After the first Bible study, she never stopped going. This college Bible study was not your basic small group; more than five hundred people attended the weekly study led by Henrietta Mears.

Doris's involvement grew and led to her even being on staff there. This is where she met her husband, Dr. Richard Halverson, the former chaplain to the U.S. Senate. As a couple they helped lead the highly influential Fourth Presbyterian Church in Bethesda, Maryland.

The Sunday school program at First Presbyterian, developed by Henrietta Mears, grew to an enrollment of six thousand, and by the 1950s was the largest in the world. She also founded a Sunday school publishing house (Gospel Light), pioneered a Christian conference center (Forest Home), and brought together the Hollywood Christian Group (for celebrities). Her books have been translated and published in more than a hundred languages around the world.

Henrietta Mears influenced hundreds of ministry leaders, including Dr. Billy Graham, Dr. Bill and Vonette Bright, Rev. Louis H. Evans, Dr. Lloyd Ogilvy, and Dr. Paul Cedar. The list reads like a who's who of evangelical leaders in America. These people are responsible for changing the lives of people in America and across the globe, yet the person who created the program that birthed such leaders was a woman, a Bible teacher, a mentor, and a "spiritual mother"—Henrietta Mears.

Dr. Bill Bright said it best: "Her life was one of spiritual multiplication." Only God, who knows the very number of hairs on our heads, can possibly count the number of souls that have been saved, the lives rescued, and the hearts delivered by the ministry created by this one spiritual mother. To begin counting the impact, the numbers grow quickly into the hundreds of millions and beyond.

It Began with a Statue

One spring, I was working in Washington, D.C., on a project to help promote the concerns of contemporary Christian women in media and politics. During this time the National Museum of Women's History was helping move the Portrait Monument from the basement of the Capitol building into the Rotunda. The Portrait Monument is a 8-ton statue that depicts three leaders of the abolition and suffrage movements: Lucretia Mott, Susan B. Anthony, and Elizabeth Cady Stanton. It was to be the only statue of women in this critically important place of honor in our nation's capitol.

I had heard the names of these women and generally knew the issues surrounding the 19th Amendment (which gave women the right to vote), but as I prepared to produce the ceremony for the Senate committee, the importance of these women's work was clarified to me. Research about these women revealed a history that I had never heard in school. The freedoms and values that these women struggled for have made it possible for me to be who I am today.

What did these women do? They changed the world through courage and persistence. They changed history in many ways and challenged the major social ills of their day—alcoholism, slavery, and the abridgment of women's rights. The work of Mott, Stanton, Anthony, and their colleagues gave me the right to a higher education. (Prior to the Civil War, most women could not attend colleges.) The work of these women helped change laws that barred women from owning property, having their own bank accounts, or earning a living. They helped women be viewed as more than property, and most importantly, to vote. Unfortunately, in many nations of the world, women are still treated as chattel.

These very active spiritual mothers fought for the rights of all women and for the betterment of our country, but like Moses who died before entering the promised land, these women died years before they saw women have the right to vote. Susan B. Anthony, the last to die, passed away almost fourteen years before the adoption of the 19th Amendment.

Working on this project caused all sorts of questions to stir within me.

• Who are the spiritual mothers in my life? Who have I been a spiritual mom to?

• What other contributions have women made that are not recognized?

• How does a spiritual mother impact the destiny and the lives of people in her sphere of influence—families, churches, and communities?

• Who are some of the spiritual mothers who have helped change cities, states, and nations?

• What lessons can we learn from spiritual moms who touch lives, nurture souls, and feed the spiritually hungry?

Spiritual Moms as Everyday Heroes

The more I looked for spiritual moms, the more I realized spiritual moms are everywhere! There are many women in our lives who are heroes. You have never heard of these women, though you may have met one at the grocery store or at work or at church. You will never recognize them as being heroes or people who do extraordinary things, but don't let their looks and humble manner keep you from recognizing the incredible work that they are doing for the Kingdom.

Scripture instructs older women to teach the younger (Titus 2), but spiritual moms do so much more than that. Spiritual moms care for the hurting, lonely, needy, hungry, unfortunate, forgotten, orphaned, and the destitute among us. It may not seem extraordinary. To them, giving and loving is as natural as fixing a meal. These are women who adopt, in a spiritual sense, those who are without a spiritual parent, family, or home.

Spiritual moms don't usually adopt their children by signing adoption papers. The spiritual mom will simply see the spiritual need of an individual and try to meet it. The adoptee may be a teenager, a child next door, or a person from work, church, or the supermarket. It may be someone she met through her child's sports team—or her own. The venue may be a Bible study, prayer meeting, mentoring group, accountability group, fellowship meeting, fundraiser, ladies' guild meeting, potluck supper, outreach...as many places as people meet.

The mothering can take place anywhere, but spiritual moms know that the heart of God can be felt more easily in the home. In the loving environment of a spiritual home many people discover the love, truth, kindness, faithfulness, and forgiveness of God. Having a peaceful place to go refreshes them and opens their spirits to growing in God.

What If Spiritual Mothers Never Acted?

The Call, DC, the event I described at the first of this chapter, would never have happened without the financial gift of a spiritual mother who chose to remain anonymous. When it came to making this pivotal event happen, it was a spiritual mom who put money where her faith was.

What would have happened if, in the 1930s, the elders of First Presbyterian Church in Hollywood had prevented Henrietta Mears from teaching? She taught the Word of God and discipled, and lives were changed. The Word of God does not come back void; it keeps multiplying as it is spoken and spread. The Scripture that comes to mind is, *"Sing, O barren, thou that didst not bear; break forth into singing, and cry aloud, thou that didst not travail with child: for more are the children of the desolate than the children of the married wife, saith the LORD"* (Isaiah 54:1 KJV).

If the courageous spiritual mothers who were called as abolitionists and suffragists had never stood against their culture and pushed for the rights of women, where would America be today? What would have happened if American women had accepted the lie that they didn't deserve an education, the right to own property, or the right to vote?

And what about our neighborhoods and homes? What would have happened if people never reached out to the children and teens around them? How much higher would the crime, teen pregnancy, and suicide statistics be?

As a woman, I have been blessed to have many wonderful spiritual mothers pour their love into my life. It was their love and spiritual mentoring that healed the wounds of the past and strengthened me for the future. They provided a healthy mirror so that I could look at myself and evaluate my destructive behaviors without fear. They gave me a view of myself that was draped in love, and a vision of my future illuminated with hope. They gave me the courage to change and the strength to fight for the truth. They directed my heart's affections to Christ and pointed my spiritual eyes to the Father.

Thank You, God, for giving me so many wonderful spiritual moms!

Chapter Three

Spiritual Orphans: In Need of a Mother's Blessing

Look for the spiritual orphans. The world is filled with millions of lost, hurting, and dying people. Their faces fill the television channels, and they walk the shopping malls aimlessly. They sit in the church pew next to you and live behind that six-foot privacy fence next door. They walk their dogs in the morning and are stuck in life's traffic jams. If you look behind the mask of "coolness," you can hear the lonely echoes of insecurity and frustration. If you look in their eyes, you will see the hunger for God and buried hope for eternity.

What Is a Spiritual Orphan?

A spiritual orphan is someone who has no parents who are able to function in the role of a spiritual parent for them. The believer may have come to God independent of his or her parents, or may have no living parents, or may be geographically separated from his parents by college, work, or career. Like a literal orphan, a spiritual orphan is looking for "parents" who can help guide her in her faith. Parents love, bless, teach, correct, guide, support, and listen to their kids. A spiritual orphan is looking for people who will help in the same manner. Orphans are looking for a family, and God wants them to have room in His house.

Can a biological mother be a spiritual mom? What is the difference? It was God's desire that all parents be their children's spiritual teachers. The home and family was where children were to be taught reverence for God and how to walk in faith. In God's perspective, it is more important to give children a spiritual inheritance than a financial inheritance. Unfortunately, growing up in a godly household is now the exception rather than the rule. This is why there are so many spiritual orphans today.

Many of the strong spiritual moms that I spoke with were blessed with godly mothers. Syble Griffing, wife of Pastor Olen Griffing of Antioch Oasis Fellowship, shares a few fond memories.

> My childhood was such a blessing. My dad and mom were such godly people. For decades they were elders at the Baptist church in West Texas. Every time the doors opened we were there. I remember one morning as we drove to church and watched this glorious sunrise, my momma said, "Look Syble, that is what it's going to look like when Jesus comes down from heaven."
>
> Every Saturday night, my mom would put my hair up in curlers. That became such a special time for us. Mom would use the time to teach me, tell me how pretty I was, and love on me. To this day, my mom is still my spiritual mom and best friend.
> —Syble Griffing

Unfortunately, experiences like Syble's are often the exception rather than the norm. That is why there is such a huge recruitment call going out for "Heroes of the Heart." People need to be told how special they are and how much they are loved. It makes all the difference in the world and

God's Kingdom to know who you are in Christ. St. Paul reminded his spiritual children of their identity time and time again: *"I keep asking that the God of our Lord Jesus Christ, the glorious Father, may give you the Spirit of wisdom and revelation, so that you may know him better. I pray also that the eyes of your heart may be enlightened in order that you may know the hope to which he has called you, the riches of his glorious inheritance in all the saints, and his incomparably great power for us who believe"* (Ephesians 1:17–19 NIV).

Birth of a Spirit

How does a person find God? Like the rare orchid in the rainforest, each story of faith is richly unique. In a faith-filled home, the knowledge of God is like bread on the table. But what about the child whose parents don't know Christ—how does that child learn about God? How does that young girl or boy make a decision to follow and reach out to the Maker of the universe?

It is a well-known fact that more than 80% of decisions to become a Christian occur before the age of eighteen. So how, when, and where are these decisions made? And if so many decisions for God are made at this age, why don't we see more young people in the pews?

Sometimes the child learns about God through a Sunday school lesson, a church service, or through divine revelation. Other times, the child is introduced to Jesus through a parent, friend, neighbor, relative, coach, teacher, television show, music, video, or book. There are various ways to find God, but as Scripture reminds us, faith is a gift of God, and unless God first calls a person, he or she will not be drawn to Him.

Sometimes God just introduces Himself to an adult or child through a "burning bush" experience or through a magnificent miracle. But in my case, at the age of four-and-a-half, it was simply a matter of "knowing." My earliest recollection of spiritual desire and hunger was as I was sitting next to my parents on the wooden pews at St. George's Episcopal Church in Bel Air, Maryland.

It was a few weeks before the new school year began, and we had recently moved to a Baltimore suburb. In an effort to meet new friends and families, my parents piled all four of us kids into the car to visit the nearby Episcopal Church. I remember standing on the church lawn next to my parents as they asked the priest where the children should go. I was thrilled to find out that I didn't have to go with my younger brother and sisters to the nursery. As I dramatically exclaimed, "Oh, good, I get to be in the big church with you," my parents probably thought I wanted a break from my siblings. In truth, I really wanted to be with the adults and learn more about God. I knew deep inside that He was there, loving me and watching me. I remember sitting very still, Sunday after Sunday, trying to listen and memorize every word that I heard, even the sermons.

Where did this desire come from? I don't know. Did I see this love for God's Word modeled in my own home? No. Later experiences with my paternal grandfather were times of nurturing my faith, but this hunger from an early age was a gift from God. Did I hear the audible voice of God? Not that I can recall, but I know that He revealed Himself to me as a child, and His existence was as much a fact as needing water to drink.

I was fortunate to have a faithful father, a cradle Presbyterian, who would diligently take us kids to the closest Episcopal Church (my mother's choice) for Sunday services and, when I was older, pick me up from choir practice on Wednesday nights. I was fortunate to have a dad who believed in the Ten Commandments and did the right thing by taking us kids to church when we were young.

The interesting point is that my dad has a very strong faith now, but he didn't accept Jesus into his heart until I was in college.

As I look back on the journey of faith that stretches behind me like a mountain stream, there are countless people and saints who have helped me reach the spiritual path that I now walk. The cradle of the church helped birth my faith, but there are more teachers, youth workers, pastors, priests, friends, musicians, writers, and spiritual mothers and fathers than I can ever repay. What a rich bounty of spiritual meals has been laid before me! From the home-cooked Bible study to the classic Bach-filled Easter, to the upbeat fast-food Young Life service, to the gospel-prayer service in Philadelphia, I have been fed, watered, washed down, prayed up, and blessed by the company of saints.

To think that one is self-made is such a depressing and hollow thought. To grow only on the island of self is to handicap one's potential forever. We are God-made, but our lives, successes, and talents are the results of God's grace through many people. Our lives are the product of the incredible love and sacrifice of many, many others. From family to friends, from mentors to movie stars, all of us have had many people pour themselves into us, and for this we must be thankful and grateful.

Watch the Momma!

Spiritual mothers contribute in many areas of life. From the children in their home to those in the neighborhood, to the classroom, and to the society of the future, people need more spiritual mothers. Besides teaching and changing the culture, one of the most obvious and more personal roles that a spiritual mother provides is that of a role model. A role model is more than someone we see on a television program; a role model is a mentor with a two-way relationship.

Until we know who we are, we are destined to play and experiment with different life scripts and roles on life's stage. Shakespeare was right—"All the world's a stage"—but we must remember that God lets us help coauthor the script through the choices we make. Spiritual children learn through watching others. They learn to talk, interact, work, and pray by following the examples they see around them. Anita Carson, known to many as "Momma," relates this story of being "watched at church":

> When you are a spiritual parent you have to be there 24/7 with no time off for vacations. You never know when people are watching you and learning from what you are doing. More than ten years ago, there was a young man who had been bribed into coming to our church by some friends. For over a year we would run into this young man everywhere we went, from the mall, to the grocery store and at church. It was a God connection and we just had to walk in it. This young man later told us that he was watching to see if we were the "same," in church and out, good situations and bad. He was also watching to see how Harold treated me as his wife and was learning a great deal from the way we loved and interacted. In the end, the young man met a young lady who was a strong Christian, but he told us that he chose her after watching us for more than a year.

The impact that a mother has upon her children grows from her own understanding of God. While once discussing childrearing with my friend Dawn, the issue of building self-esteem came up. Dawn said something that has always stuck with me: "I am more concerned with my daughter's 'Jesus-esteem' than her self-esteem. If Elizabeth knows who she is in Christ, then self-esteem won't be a problem." Even though Dawn survived breast cancer and a devastating divorce, which made her a single parent from the time Elizabeth was three, the fruit of this truth is obvious. Seeing Elizabeth more than fifteen years later as a radiant, confident, and gifted college student, I know that Dawn was right. As a mother, she focused on building the spiritual esteem that her daughter needed.

Moms and Identity

God is so practical in the way He teaches us. God uses the biological family to teach us about spiritual relationship. Many families consider the father as the head of the house, but the mother is considered to be the heart. Even though both parents give children love, training, care, protection, and provision, parents contribute different elements of destiny. Fathers give children their family name, which is like the "tribe" or a heritage. This gives a person her place and purpose.

Children's first bonding relationship is with their mother, whom they must depend upon for food, protection, and care. Even from the womb children sense love, blessing, and that they are wanted. Mothers give children unconditional love, which gives children a sense of identity, which helps to build individuality.

A Mother's Blessing

In Scripture, Abraham, Isaac, and many other fathers would pray blessings upon their sons. This was critically important and spiritually significant, but what about the blessings mothers gave to their families and daughters? Even though there is no official tradition of mother's blessings in the Bible, there are several times in Scripture when women spoke blessings. One great example is in the story of Ruth, when the women of the village say to Naomi, when Ruth gives birth to a son, that Ruth is better to Naomi than seven sons! Considering how important sons were in those days, this is an incredible blessing and testimony to Ruth's worth.

Blessing was meant by God to be a part of our daily life. As we look at Jewish traditions, we can learn more of what the Lord wanted in family interaction. In the Jewish custom, the children stay under the mother's tutelage until they are twelve years old. In those twelve years the mother is to love, teach, and speak into the lives of her children. Today, with so many fractured families, this often does not happen—there is a serious lack of parental teaching and blessing. That is why spiritual moms have to help fill the need. Anita Carson shares again:

> There are people who have never had a mother embrace them and tell them how proud they are of them. There are so many people that are so wounded by the world, and all they have heard are things like, "I didn't want you," and "You are worthless."
>
> I tell them that they are good. If it is a woman, I tell her, "You are a good daughter." If it is a man, "You are a good son!" A Momma needs to tell children that they are good.

Once a person feels acceptance from her mother, she is then able to receive the love and correction from the father. There is no age limit to the need for affirmation from a spiritual parent. The important principle is that both the father's and mother's blessings and prayers are critical to a person's well being. There is nothing like a word of praise to light up a person's face and touch the soul.

Keep the Sabbath Holy

Another Jewish tradition teaches us principles and patterns of blessings. At the traditional Friday night Sabbath meal, it is the wife who prays over the candles at the beginning of the Sabbath. The first prayer of the evening comes from the mother, a prayer that invites the presence of God and prepares the way spiritually. At the end of the meal it is tradition that the father prays over his children and blesses them because they are his children. What a wonderful thing it is to have blessings spoken over you by your parents every Friday night.

Have you ever attended a Sabbath meal or Passover with messianic believers? Do it sometime! You will be amazed at how much you learn. Also, I encourage you to practice speaking blessings over the lives of your children, spouse, and friends, who gather with you. Our fellowship group meets monthly for Friday night fellowships. We have a meal, take communion, have a time of study, pray, and speak blessings over each other. It is always a memorable evening.

With this tradition in mind, one wonders what happened when Jesus celebrated the Sabbath. Can you imagine what it would have been like to have Jesus, the living Word, look into your eyes and speak a blessing over you each Friday? No wonder the disciples always looked forward to the Sabbath!

In Jesus' ministry, at the weekly Sabbath, I wonder which women were given the honor and responsibility of praying over the candles and inviting God's presence to join them? Scripture doesn't tell us, but I wonder if Jesus, at the end of the meal, spoke blessing over each person before He walked to the garden of Gethsemane?

The Story of Two Trees

I have two trees in my front yard. One of them is planted near the driveway, between several sprinkler heads. The other is on a hill, which causes the water to run off quickly.

Even though they were the same size when they were planted, now, after four years, in spite of equal watering and care, the tree next to the driveway is much healthier than the one on the slope.

The stunted growth of the tree is similar to the growth of the human soul. Love is like water to the heart. Praise, encouragement, and acknowledgement help feed the soul, heart, and spirit of a person. In every letter he wrote, St. Paul always thanked God for his spiritual children, and he offered his prayers, encouragement, and praise.

So much of what we are depends on how our parents and role models interact with us. Even though our parents may be loving, intelligent, and well meaning, sometimes conflicts, wounds, and issues prevent them from giving their children the direction that they need. In my situation, because of divorce and personal issues, our parents were unable to instill in us kids a healthy self-image when we were at a critical stage in our lives.

For balance, it is important to stress that our family situation still produced great blessings, and we had terrific opportunities growing up. Our parents did love us, and they made great sacrifices to provide us with a good education, moral values, social skills, and an appreciation for art and culture. Dad's keen mind and love of history, mathematics, and education gave us structure. Mom gave us a love for beauty and home. She comes from a family of gifted artists and is the most remarkable craftsperson I have ever seen. We all have good memories mixed with the pain from the past, but my siblings and I were somewhat relieved when our parents divorced.

The pain of the past was the true culprit that destroyed their marriage. Without the forgiveness and healing love of God, unresolved emotional pain became a thief that stole the future. Without Christ at the center of any marriage, overcoming the challenges of life can be difficult if not impossible. Bitterness is like a fast-growing vine that will block all light and twist truth in any relationship. Unfortunately, my parents found themselves in an emotional jungle where they believed that their only hope for survival was to extract themselves as quickly as possible.

The Story of Two Sisters

When there are holes in a bucket, it doesn't hold water very well. The same is true with faith and beliefs. If your spirit has holes in it of doubt or despair, then you can't hold on to whatever's poured into it. Without the belief that you are lovable, you will not be able to receive love. Without the belief that you are a blessing, you will not be able to accept blessings. Without the faith that God loves you, you will not be able to accept His love and forgiveness. Divorce is a major enemy that has robbed our world of both natural and spiritual parents and left millions of children and adults in physical and spiritual poverty.

Since our parents' divorce, my sister Catherine and I have moved from total alienation to a deep friendship. As the older sister, I tended to boss around my grown sister, who justifiably resented it. There was a typical sister conflict between us. Conversations would explode into sharp words and months of silence. But as we have matured, we both worked to change. In the past few years we have both gone through counseling and inner healing and have prayed to develop our relationship.

One day as we were on the phone, Catherine was sharing about her work success in handling a person of difficult character. It was then that I realized that she needed to hear how proud I was of her and what she was doing. As the third-born middle child, with a younger handicapped sister, she had never received the attention, encouragement, and support that she needed. As a girl, Catherine hadn't been told how wonderful and special she was. She hadn't been praised and blessed enough. As an adult, Catherine still hadn't received the affirmation she deserved. My sister needed to hear how terrific she was, that I loved her, that she was important to me, and that she was acting in a godly manner. My sister needed a mother's blessing!

So I blessed her. I told Catherine what every person's heart and spirit needs to hear. I told her all the things that she needed to hear years ago at a time when my mother was unable to tell her so. And best of all, my sister really heard me! She responded, and our relationship and love for each other continues to grow. There is nothing like a laugh with my sister to make me smile for days. Our relationship has been healed and continues to grow because I was able to give my sister a "mom's blessing" at a critical time. We now take turns blessing each other, and it's such a delight.

Spiritual moms play an important role in blessing God's children. You are never too old to get a hug and to hear words of acceptance and words like, *I love you, I am proud of you, you are God's child and you are good.* This love and acceptance helps to heal the soul and opens the way so that people can then grow in faith. Everyone, everywhere, needs a mother's blessing all the time. Like the rain, blessings help make the seeds grow.

Jean Crisler Wilford— Divine Blessings from My Mom

The fifth commandment, to honor your father and mother, is the only commandment that is followed by a promise: *"so that you may live long in the land that the LORD your God is giving you."* In a book honoring spiritual moms, it is important to me that I honor my biological mother, Jean Wilford, and share one of the great surprises God gave me through her. For God does know the plans He has for us, even though we are often clueless about them.

Mother always told me the same thing her mother told her, that when I got older I would appreciate my parents more. They both were right. Age has a way of rubbing off the shell of pride and ego that we take on in youth. Growing up, even though we loved each other, the differences of our worldviews and faith put an emotional valley between us. But Jesus is truly the bridge of life, and His love can transcend even the grandest canyon.

As we grew up, our parents provided us kids with great education, opportunities, valuable life skills, and experiences. I am blessed to have been given parents who believed in me and sacrificed time and time again to help me in times of crisis and career roadblocks. Having a family that has been there in the dark and difficult times is one of the greatest blessings of my life.

Until I was in high school, I was the only believer in my family. Regardless of that fact, as I was growing up I wished for a mom who taught Bible study, or parents who would share my enthusiasm for the gospel. After my parents divorced, like many families, we were scattered to the wind. College, jobs, and work assignments spread us apart. At the age of 50, my mom joined the U.S. State Department and for more than 12 years was stationed in faraway countries, often in volatile circumstances. Many times Mom invited me to visit. Circumstances, finances, and work kept me from going, but in truth these were excuses that covered my ignorance, pride, and fear—fear that kept me from experiencing these countries and cultures.

Spiritual Inheritance

Over the last decade, my heart for ministry has shifted focus toward people in Third World nations. One day, while pondering where this intense concern came from, I noticed I was wearing a scarf that my mom had sent me from India. As I considered all the places my mom had lived, these were the same places that now make my heart cry out and swell with love and compassion for the people. God had used my mother to cut a path toward my spiritual destiny.

It hit me like brick: for years, through Mom's life and experiences, God was preparing a spiritual inheritance for me and shaping a spiritual destiny that neither of us realized. While Mom may not have understood the measure and dimension of my faith walk, there were still deeper and more important things that God was doing through her life to develop my heart and prepare me for future missions around the world. I had to repent.

A Joseph's Coat

Not long afterward I visited my mom and told her that God had shown me that I needed to ask her forgiveness. I told her how God had been shaping my life. I told her how much I appreciated all that she had taught me through living in places like Iraq, India, Brunei, and Turkey. My mother had a love for these people and countries that were now being transferred to my heart. Like Joseph's "robe of many colors," all the presents, crafts, and pictures she had given me over the years were being woven into a garment of ministry. Mom taught me lessons that helped me be better equipped. Mom had a love for many of these people and their cultures before my spiritual eyes were turned in that direction.

Who would have ever dreamed that God would have used my mother to shape my spiritual destiny as an adult? God honored my mother regardless of our spiritual differences. Through my mother the Lord is allowing me to inherit gifts and blessings that will be used to fulfill the Great Commission.

Blessings Multiplied

My mom has always helped me bless others. I always keep an overpacked business schedule, and Mom helps me out in wonderful ways, especially with client presents at Christmas. This is a major undertaking, as I love giving homemade gifts like spice blends, jams, vinegars, pesto, cakes, and cookies. In addition to being an incredible craftsperson, my mom is a fabulous gardener and cook. So to help me out, Mom spends countless hours drying herbs and mailing them to me. Her herbs have a much better flavor than the store-bought variety. People really love our spice blends, and we wonder what the future holds for us there.

It is symbolic that spice blends are the signature gift from mom and me. It's as if God has taken all our experiences—sweet, bitter, and spicy—and mixed them together in love so that they bless others. They say that love is the spice of life, but when it is mixed with God's grace we never know what flavor it will be.

The way my mom supports me in my gift giving is such a perfect example of what moms and spiritual moms do. Moms help their children to use their gifts—physical, mental, and spiritual—to reach out to the world. Moms sacrifice themselves and empower their children to do more than they ever could. As for my mom and me, my prayer is that through the gifts we create people will "taste the love," be fed spiritually, and experience the goodness of God.

The Four Seasons

Chapter Four

The Four Seasons of the Christian Life

There is a time for everything,
and a season for every activity under heaven:
a time to be born and a time to die,
a time to plant and a time to uproot.
—Ecclesiastes 3:1–2 NIV

What do spiritual moms do? Lots of times it just depends on the season. In life there are many seasons. Just as a mom helps her child through all the stages into adulthood, spiritual moms do the same for the children of God. In the last section of this book, we learned how to spot a spiritual mom and how to be one. How many characteristics did you find in your life? Did you discover that you are a spiritual mom and you didn't even realize it? In this section, we will discuss the role of spiritual moms and how they meet the needs of people in each season of their Christian walk.

Know the Season

It was a cool early autumn day and perfect for working in the garden. The front flowerbeds were looking a bit ragged, and most of the flowers had been cooked by the summer sun or eaten as appetizers by the rampant grasshoppers, unaffected by the sprays and powders that were supposed to kill them. Houseguests were coming at the end of the month, so I dropped by the nursery to see what flowers were available for immediate planting. To my surprise, the normally packed tables were empty and the aisles of this garden oasis were deserted.

A young man in a brown apron gave me the lowdown. "Ma'am, we don't really have anything in right now. Anything you plant now won't make it through the fall. It is transition time, so why don't you just come back in a couple of weeks." Not the best job of selling I've ever seen, but he was honest. Too bad, because if he had read my body language he would have known that I was in a mood to toss some dirt around. The garden needed a facelift, and today seemed like a fine time to start.

Acknowledging the futility of my search, I surrendered to the rules of the season and returned home. As I walked by the flowerbeds on the way to my front door, I noticed that there were several bluebonnet plants growing where zinnias had been planted. This was unusual, as it wasn't the season for them.

Bluebonnets are a small, native lupine and are the state flower of Texas, where I live. In the early spring, bluebonnets grow wild along the roadways. They cover the fields with a blue and purple quilt that gives off a wonderful fragrance when you stand in them knee deep. But here it was September and the bluebonnets by my door kept getting larger and larger. Those plants were about six months off schedule. The cooler summer with extra rain must have confused them. I knew that they wouldn't make it through the fall, so I made a mental note to transplant them into a pot and see if they would bloom inside.

Know the Needs

Our lives are filled with different seasons and cycles of growth. We must know what season we are in personally, professionally, and spiritually. Once you understand the season it is easier to set goals and build accomplishments.

Being a spiritual mother is a call and an expression of God's gifts. Like all spiritual gifts, they are expressed in different seasons and in response to different needs. There are times when you dig in the garden and times when you pick flowers. Sometimes it takes years and sometimes a simple word will move mountains.

Paul wrote in his letter to the Corinthians: *"I planted the seed, Apollos watered it, but God made it grow"* (1 Corinthians 3:6 NIV). It is obvious that growth is attributed to God, but people have different jobs to do. If a spiritual mom wrote this today, it might read: "Marilyn is the one who prayed with you. Teresa taught your Bible study. Cynthia brought the casseroles when you were sick. Carol spent time on the phone when you needed advice in your marriage. Karen lent you a printer, and Joan remembered your birthday. Nora helped you clean the house, and Wendy took care of your toddler while you were in church. But it was God who wooed you to Him and gave His Son, who shed His light into your heart and helped you to change. God called you when you were lost; these spiritual moms and sisters helped you find Him."

All Talents Count!

In the Bible, a talent is a term for a coin or measure of money. In our world we think of talents as extraordinary gifts that put people in the spotlight and lead to fame or fortune. But it is better to return to the original meaning of talent, as something that everyone has and everyone uses.

Like quarters in your pocket, your talents are waiting to be used. All of us have talent and value in God's Kingdom. God is just waiting for us to remember that we have them and can cash them in for the Kingdom.

Women often discount the value of their gifts because in the home they are not given a dollar value. Noted financial analyst Sylvia Porter has calculated that the labor performed by a mom would cost a family between $23,000–26,000 a year for just the menial jobs. Porter says that the government should give moms a medal for productivity.

It is important that spiritual moms are also recognized and cherished. Spiritual moms often don't see that what they are doing is important because they love doing it. It is just a natural reaction and they love helping people. But it is important to know that every gift, action, and service for the Lord is important. It is important that we not compare ourselves to others because God has designed us each for His own purposes. Paul reminds us, *"There should be no division in the body, but that its parts should have equal concern for each other. If one part suffers, every part suffers with it; if one part is honored, every part rejoices with it"* (1 Corinthians 12:25–26 NIV).

But the bottom line is, we have no way of measuring the value of our actions and words to God. Little things mean a lot in the Kingdom. Every talent counts, so get your talents out of your pockets and start using them. No matter how small, every action that a person does for the Lord is important and valuable.

People grow fastest in an environment of love. That is why the Lord gave us families on earth and has brought us into His family. Spiritual mothers and fathers are the Lord's way of bringing more spiritual children into the kingdom.

Four Seasons of Growth

So what does a spiritual mom do? Just like a natural mom, she does too many things to count. A mother adapts to the needs of her children, and so does a spiritual mom. In evaluating the different types of spiritual mothering, there seem to be several categories that relate to the stages or "seasons" of people's needs. These categories are analogies, developed from my experience as a spiritual mom and daughter, and help to identify the stages of a person's spiritual walk and the roles that spiritual moms fulfill.

Season	Spiritual Mom's Role
1. Seed	Nurture, Love, Touch, Affirm, Bless, Come Alongside
2. Feed	Teach, Tend, Mend, Build Relationships, Strengthen
3. Weed	Prune, Build Discipline, Build Character, Pray, Worship
4. Lead	Equip to Lead, Minister, Release to the Call

The Seed Season: Salvation and Early Growth

Mothers are equipped to love a baby even when its diaper is messy and it has food all over its face. Moms aren't upset when things seem confusing and out of control. Moms know how to roll up their sleeves and get to work to straighten up a dirty kitchen or a difficult past. Spiritual moms are equipped by God to handle the task of caring for the new believers and assimilating them into the community.

It takes time for a new believer to become a mature person of faith. It also takes lots of work and the effort of many people. Yes, it takes a full church to raise a believer. That's what body ministry really means. The church family is God's incubator. Spiritual moms are critical in the formative days, weeks, and years of a new believer's spiritual walk.

Unfortunately, too many spiritual newborns starve to death after being born again because there aren't enough people to help feed, hold, and direct them. Growing churches know how to plug a new believer in quickly. Jesus warned about these problems with the parable of the sower, where a large portion of the seed sown never yields a crop.

The farmer sows the seed of the gospel. Some people are like soil along the path, where the Word is sown. As soon as they hear it, Satan comes and takes away the word that was sown in them. Others, like soil in rocky places, hear the Word and at once receive it with joy. But since it doesn't take root, it lasts only a short time. When trouble or persecution comes because of the Word, they quickly fall away. Still others, like soil that is covered with thorns, hear the Word but the worries of this life come in and choke the Word, making it unfruitful. Others, like good soil, hear the Word, accept it, and produce a crop thirty, sixty, or even a hundred times what was sown (based on Mark 4:3–20).

In this parable, it seems that more than 75% of the seed was unfruitful. Dr. Edwin Louis Cole stated, "The culture is the culprit in the loss of this seed." Like a child who doesn't know how to care for or feed himself, there are too many people who do not grow in their Christian faith because of a lack of knowledge. This could be remedied with the simple guidance of a spiritual mom.

When the enemy attempts to snatch away a seed, a spiritual mom can help ease doubts and fears. When the seed is in danger of withering for lack of root, spiritual moms can help ground a person's faith. When the fruit is choked by the cares of the world, a spiritual mom can protect a new believer by sharing wisdom and knowledge.

The Feed Season: Tending the Lambs

"Feed my lambs" (John 21:15 NIV). The last time Jesus appeared to the disciples, Jesus instructed Peter to feed and tend His lambs. The second stage of growth in a believer's life is like the elementary age school child who has lots of energy but is always hungry and bumping into things. In this stage, they need to be taught basic rules, manners, and how to get along with other children.

In the church today there are thousands of "spiritual newborns" who are dying for lack of spiritual food. Likewise, there are too many Christians who never get the candles on their two-year cake because they fall away from the faith due to insufficient spiritual instruction, discipline, and guidance.

In this stage of growth, spiritual moms are helping to feed, tend, and heal people on both personal and spiritual levels. Spiritual moms help to feed the flock through teaching the basics of Bible study, prayer, Scripture memory, service, and character development. The home is the most effective environment a spiritual mom has. Why? Because when you are invited into a spiritual mom's home, you step into her heart and are surrounded by love.

All of my spiritual mothers invited me into their homes and wooed me further into the Kingdom, and it is now through *my* home that I find myself functioning as a spiritual mom most often. Though I also spend thousands of hours with people in other cities, it is mainly through my home—over a meal—that most counsel has been given, prayers prayed, and lives shared.

The Weed Season: Weeding and Pruning Back

"I am the true vine, and my Father is the gardener. He cuts off every branch in me that bears no fruit, while every branch that does bear fruit he prunes so that it will be even more fruitful" (John 15:1–2 NIV). This third stage of a believer's life is similar to adolescence, when young men and women are growing rapidly, are always hungry, get distracted easily, have lots of emotional ups and downs, have tremendous energy, and are trying to figure out who they are. They have great passion and need encouragement to make it through discouragement and fear.

In this stage, spiritual moms help to discipline, strengthen, and direct a person's energies. Like teens, their children must learn to walk and run on their own and cultivate the disciplines of Bible study, worship, prayer, and service to others. This is like the boot camp stage for Christian soldiers. Sometimes a person needs a push instead of a hug to finish the race. As the Lord uses the hills and valleys of our life to strengthen our walk, this stage is often filled with great highs and lows that test faith. Some people need help to make it through the valleys and challenges of a deeper walk with Christ.

In John 15 Jesus describes Himself as the vine and believers as the branches. God, as the vinedresser, not only prunes off the unproductive branches, but He prunes the productive vines so they might yield even more fruit. Following God's example, spiritual parents need to be concerned about the fruitfulness of the lives of those they teach.

Even though God makes the fruit grow, spiritual moms and dads contribute to a successful harvest. The spiritual fruit in our lives is meant to feed a starving world, nourish the weak, feed the needy, refresh the warrior, nurse the ill, sustain the righteous, energize the intercessor, and bless the elders and pastors.

The Lead Season: Release Them to God's Call

"Therefore go and make disciples of all nations" (Matthew 28:19 NIV). The desire of all parents, mentors, teachers, and businesspeople is for their children and those they have trained to launch out into the world and have successful lives. Whether in college, career, military, marriage, or ministry, people must be prepared for the challenges ahead of them. Spiritual moms many times say that their spiritual children are doing things that they never dreamed of, and that is exactly what they hoped and prayed for.

At this final stage, spiritual moms are called to help lead people into their destiny and then release them. Sometimes it takes a little push and sometimes it takes several shoves to get people to jump out of the boat and walk on the water of life.

Leadership requires vision, and spiritual moms know how to cast vision and turn the spotlight of truth on the future. Finally, spiritual moms know that being in a person's corner is the greatest reassurance of all. Spiritual moms know that even though a spiritual child may launch into the unknown, she will be back eventually to share the testimonies of how God was real in her life.

Spiritual Moms Defy the Rules

Here are a few observations about spiritual moms that defy the normal rules of the traditional family and physical world:

1. You can have more than one mom! This is great news. I have many spiritual moms, which either says that I am fortunate or that I have needed them or both. Each of my spiritual moms has been there for me in different seasons of my life and stages of my growth. Mother's Day is a very busy time for the mailman around my house.

2. Different needs, different moms. Spiritual moms are wonderfully able to adapt to the needs of their children. Just as a mom can multitask in the kitchen, so a spiritual mom is able to change hats faster than a bargain hunter at Neiman Marcus. It all depends upon understanding what the needs of a person are and which you are to meet at which time.

Multitasking is very much a female gift, but one for which I am very grateful. A normal mom is able to answer the phone, start lunch, suggest a game for the kids, load the dishwasher, pour a drink, make the grocery list, stop the fight over the crayons, let the dog out, and glance at the news all in a time frame of about ten minutes, and that is a slow day!

3. Every relationship is unique—different rules for different people! All relationships are different because every person is different. Some spiritual moms may bond with a person for a lifetime, like Naomi and Ruth, and others may only be in a person's life for a season. Some may be in a formal mentoring situation like Elijah and Elisha, and others may be long distance relationships with occasional phone calls.

4. Childless women often make great spiritual moms. You don't have to be a physical mom to be a spiritual mom. Remember, all of God's children's are adopted in and born of the Spirit and truth. I interviewed many women who were active spiritual moms who had never had children.

God places inside each woman all the ingredients to be a mom, physically and spiritually. Just watch little girls and how they play with their dolls and take care of their needs. Nurturing is the very core of a woman's personality. When God touches your spiritual womb, there is no limit to what you can do.

5. Age doesn't matter. Spiritual parents are usually older biologically than their spiritual children, but this is not a hard and fast rule. Even though my spiritual moms are older than I am, and the majority of my spiritual daughters/sons are young enough to be my kids, some of my spiritual "children" have been thirty and forty years older than I am. Several women and men pointed out the critical need for spiritual parenting of the elderly and those in nursing homes who don't know Christ. This is a prison for many who are lonely and depressed, and they are so appreciative of a kind word and prayer.

I find it best to follow the same instructions that Paul gave Timothy, which taught him how to be a spiritual parent, leading and teaching those adults who were older than he was. Paul also reminded him not to be intimidated or fearful about his age but to ask God to stir up the gifts within him (2 Timothy 1:6). This is a good reminder that we are not to be intimidated by a person's biological age, but instead we need to let our gifts be used freely by God whenever and however He chooses.

6. Spiritual parenting is not limited to women. Men can also "spiritually parent" a person. Spiritual fruit is not gender specific. For me, my paternal grandfather was my first spiritual parent. During our summer vacations in New Hampshire, I was refreshed personally and spiritually as my "Pop-pop" would pour into my life. When we drove around in his 1930 Franklin, we would sing his favorite hymns. When we went fishing he would tell me about the Lord's Prayer and the Beatitudes. On Sundays we would go to the wooden white Baptist church and we would nudge him in case he started to sing a bit too loud or off key. What my grandfather did was encourage my faith as a child. He taught me to love the Lord, study the Word, and sing at the top of my lungs when you don't know the words.

7. Time and space don't matter. In the electronic age, time and space have become less relevant. Television, cell phones, radio, the Internet, and other technologies have changed the way we learn and grow. Spiritual moms can teach through a book, tape, radio show, or a daily television broadcast. There are spiritual moms all over the airwaves, helping equip women all over the world.

On a simpler model, the phone and the Internet are great tools, also. Marge Caldwell, who is Beth Moore's spiritual mom, tells how she and her husband met a woman whom she had been counseling long distance for over five years. The woman had contacted Marge after hearing her speak at a conference. Over the years they wrote and spoke on the phone. Finally, on a trip to Oklahoma for a conference, Marge and her husband, Chuck, met the woman in the airport. "We all hugged and talked like we were old friends. Even though I had never met her face-to-face, because of our spiritual relationship we were able to have a great time."

8. There's always room for one more. Just as you can always learn from a good teacher, you can always learn from a great spiritual mom. In my life, some of the spiritual moms have been there for a few months and others have been there for decades. The great news is that just as there is always room for one more for dinner, so there is always room for one or two or a dozen more "kiddos" in the heart of a spiritual mom.

Spiritual moms are willing to love, teach, and counsel scores of people. It seems that the more they love, the bigger their hearts grow. This is an amazing characteristic of the heart. Its ability to expand with love and affection is almost endless. Of course, with God as the source of love, it makes it easy. When He pours love through a spiritual mom there is an infinite supply.

Spiritual moms are found in all the seasons of a believer's life. They protect the seeds, feed new believers, weed out distractions, and lead Christians into great fruitfulness for the Kingdom. Spiritual moms reach across age, distance, and time to touch the lives and hearts of those entrusted to them by heaven.

Chapter Five

The Seed Season: Salvation and Early Growth

Christ has no body now on earth but yours,
no hands but yours, no feet but yours;
yours are the eyes through which Christ's compassion
looks out on the world,
yours are the feet with which He is to go about doing good
and yours are the hands with which He is to bless us now.
—Teresa of Avila

There are thousands of details and checklists that must be handled before a space shuttle takes off. And as we learned tragically with the space shuttle Columbia, even the simplest problem ignored can strip the protective covering off a billion dollar vehicle.

One of the standard and final procedures that occur before the astronauts go into space is that they fill out papers that are only opened in the case of emergency. In the Columbia packet left by Commander Rick Husband was a handwritten note to his pastor, Steve Riggle of Grace Community Church in Houston. In his last hours on earth, Commander Husband wrote: "Pastor Steve, tell them about Jesus. He was real to me!"

Make Jesus Real

That is what God has called us to do. It is a very simple request. So simple that we often forget—so powerful that when we experience the "realness of Jesus" in our lives, it changes us. It is so strong that the life inside of one person can transform a community. Centuries ago, Saint Teresa of Avila wrote,

> Christ has no body now on earth but yours,
> no hands but yours, no feet but yours;
> yours are the eyes through which Christ's compassion
> looks out on the world,
> yours are the feet with which He is to go about doing good
> and yours are the hands with which He is to bless us now.

Spiritual moms and dads are those people who make Jesus real. They do it in a million ways and often without even realizing what they have done. A spiritual mom provides a touch point, a safe place, a warm hug, a word of encouragement, a bright smile, and a walking blessing in the lives of those around them, especially in the "seed stage."

As we discussed in the last chapter, there are four major seasons of spiritual growth: Seed, Feed, Weed, and Lead. This chapter is about the Seed season, which forms the beginning steps of a person's faith.

The Seed stage is a time around a person's salvation, which requires a great deal of care and one-on-one attention. Let's look again at the parable of the sower, found in Mark 4:2–20:

> "Listen! A farmer went out to sow his seed. As he was scattering the seed, some fell along the path, and the birds came and ate it up. Some fell on rocky places, where it did not have much soil. It sprang up quickly, because the soil was shallow. But when the sun came up, the plants were

scorched, and they withered because they had no root. Other seed fell among thorns, which grew up and choked the plants, so that they did not bear grain. Still other seed fell on good soil. It came up, grew and produced a crop, multiplying thirty, sixty, or even a hundred times."

Then Jesus said, "He who has ears to hear, let him hear."
—Mark 4:3–9 NIV

The seed, which represents the Word of the gospel, never grows to fruitfulness when it is snatched away, dried up, or choked out by worries and distractions. Spiritual moms help to make sure that a person's seed of faith makes it into the good soil, gets water, develops roots, and has a chance to grow to completion.

The Seed season requires special attention to the individual soul. The areas that a spiritual mom helps with are:
• **Touch 'em**
• **Love 'em**
• **Tell 'em**
• **Bless 'em**

Talking About Seed

Physical children are conceived from physical seed. Spiritual children are conceived from spiritual seed. This is what Jesus meant when He said, *"Unless one is born again, he cannot see the kingdom of God....that which is born of the Spirit is spirit"* (John 3:3, 6 NKJV).

What is "spiritual seed"? Spiritual seed is the Word of God, seed that is planted in the human heart and finds root in the spirit of a man or woman.

How does it get planted? *"Faith comes from hearing the message, and the message is heard through the word of Christ"* (Romans 10:17 NIV). This means that when people hear God's Word it is able to be planted. They receive in faith and believe. Some people hear the Word, others read it, and many see it living through the saints.

God has called us to broadcast His spiritual seed, the living Word, into the lives of others. When we speak God's Word, we plant God's seed. When we speak the living Word, we speak Jesus. We must think of our words as powerful little packages that inject Jesus into people's lives. Like a fuse on a bomb, God's words can set off explosions inside people's hearts and spirits.

First, let's consider the challenges and accomplishments that are going on for the gospel in the world today. A tremendous amount of spiritual seed has been planted in America. Most adults over the age of thirty have heard the gospel message. In comparison to the rest of the world, America has multiple resources that may be tapped to hear God's Word, yet the harvest isn't proportionate to what has been planted. This spiritual seed has been and is being paid for with great sacrifice. We need to insure that this costly seed isn't snatched, withered, or choked by the enemy. Spiritual moms, through an incredible time commitment and a generosity of spirit, increase the odds of successful cultivation.

Unfortunately, the western philosophy of seeking quantity rather than quality and "notches on the baptismal font" has created an imbalance in our churches. Some of the disturbing questions include:

• If there are so many professing Christians in America, why aren't the churches full?
• Why is there such a high attrition rate after salvation in so many of our churches?
• Why are there so many prodigals?
• Why do so many people accept the Lord yet quickly fall back into the same old behavior patterns?
• If a company experienced the same attrition rate as

churches, wouldn't it undertake a serious evaluation of its business practices?

Growing churches show increased layperson involvement. In these churches where people are involved and released into fulfilling their destiny in Christ, church growth is stronger, church membership is more fulfilling, and giving increases. But whether or not a person becomes involved depends upon whether he feels accepted and on someone taking the time to reach out and take his hand and say, "Join us, won't you?"

Touch 'Em

I was out walking recently and came across a puppy that was running loose along the walking path. It was cold, scared, and quickly ran to me when I called. My mothering instinct rose up to protect this cute little beagle-dachshund mutt. I put it on a leash and took it home, where it disrupted the entire day, but it was worth every minute. One look at those sweet brown eyes that were so appreciative of every scratch and treat and I had to respond. Well, it's easy to get the picture.

Would you leave a newborn chick, kitten, or puppy to fend for itself, knowing that without shelter or food it would die? Yet in the Christian world today, too many spiritual newborns are dying because of lack of touch, affection, and care. Unfortunately it's hard to recognize them because they often hide behind cool masks of "I'm okay" and "I'm fine."

Spiritual moms are critical to spiritual growth, especially in the early stages of a newborn spirit. Study after study reports that the biological mother's influence greatly impacts the immediate and long-term success of a child. Every physical, emotional, intellectual, developmental, and relational need is usually satisfied by mother's love and care. It is the mother who speaks to the child before he can talk back, knows intuitively the need for food or changing, responds to cries and laughter. A mother cradles the child who is afraid and will fight to the death to protect her offspring from danger. A mother cares for an infant until he can walk, feeds him until he can feed himself, talks to him even when he can't speak, and models behaviors until he learns how to accomplish the hundreds of skills necessary for survival.

The critical importance of a mother to an infant's well being has been tested, often tragically. In the thirteenth century, Salimbene wrote of the attempt of King Frederick II to raise children without maternal affection:

> He wanted to find out what kind of speech children would have when they grew up if they spoke to no one beforehand. So he bade foster mothers and nurses to suckle the children, to bathe and wash them, but in no way to prattle with them, or to speak to them, for he wanted to learn whether they would speak the Hebrew language, which was the oldest, or Greek, or Latin, or Arabic, or perhaps the language of their parents, of whom they had been born. But he labored in vain, because the children all died. For they could not live without the petting and joyful faces and loving words of their foster mothers.

It doesn't take a tragic test like Frederick's to explain how much a baby needs its mother. Research constantly affirms the importance of a mother in the formative years of a child's life. Touching improves the health of newborns, and increased stimulation of the infant seems to affect future IQ levels. Healthy and frequent interaction impacts self-esteem and self-discipline, and recent studies show that a child's success in school is related to the IQ level of the mother.

These psychological principles are also true for spiritual children as well, regardless of biological age. Experts in church growth report that the sooner a new believer can become involved in a small group where they form personal relationships, the greater their chances are for long-term church membership. Spiritual IQ also depends upon the Bible study training and encouragement that a new convert receives.

"There is no age limit to the need for a Momma hug and affirmation," states Anita Carson, who is a 70-year-old spiritual mom to people in Dallas, the Ukraine, British Columbia, and Burkina Faso in West Africa. "Being a spiritual mom means being available. You have to be willing to give a hug to anyone who needs it regardless of who they are or what they look like. I have given out Momma hugs to many that normally I wouldn't want to hug because they don't look nice or smell so good. They may have just gotten off working the night shift and came to church, tired, lonely, and needy."

"It is important to just spend some down time with people," shares Syble Griffing. "For the women we do sleepovers and stay up all night playing games, cards, and just talking."

Carolyn O'Neal has an entire Sunday school class of women to interact with at First Baptist Church in Houston. Carolyn tries to give as much attention to and have as much contact with as many women as she can. "One day I walked by one woman and touched her on the back and gave her a simple pat on the shoulder. She wrote me a letter that I will never know what that pat meant to her. It was just a pat."

Carolyn shares that each person is different and you have to adjust. "Another woman didn't want to be touched and I had to ask permission to touch or hug her, where another young gal would always wait to give me a hug.

This young woman is strong and after she hugs me there is no doubt that you have been hugged. Many people come to church wanting you to touch them and when you touch them they feel loved."

Love 'Em

Love is the coin of the Kingdom. Carolyn O'Neal says, "If you make a difference in one person's life you have made a difference in the Kingdom. It is my greatest desire for women to be all they can be. They just don't know what that is. You just need to know that someone believes in you."

Love is what we need and what we want more than anything. Love is the coin of God's Kingdom. Love is the measure of our lives and the foundation of our hope. Love is the greatest of "these" and the best gift that we can ever give.

The Kingdom of God is built one soul at a time. Sometimes it takes a lot of love, attention, care, and energy to get those souls ready to even hear the gospel.

Spiritual moms understand love and have learned how to express it in millions of creative ways. Like the sunlight on the garden, love makes things grow and bear fruit. It is the joy of seeing people grow and produce a good harvest that keeps spiritual moms going.

Macy Domingo, a TV and radio talk show host from Cote d'Ivoire, says, "I am a mother-in-Christ for ten young ladies from all walks of life. One is a doctor, another a professor, another a housewife, and one sells vegetables in the market. All of them call me mommy and I am very close to all of them. For those who live in the same city, they will sometimes call me two or three times a day for advice or counsel. They all know that I love them very much."

Tell 'Em

People often don't know who they are. As women it is even more difficult because our culture tries especially hard to shape us into its image. God promises to renew our minds, but it takes time. The question that we all have to ask the Lord is, "Who do You say I am?" This is a very big question for the person who is just beginning their faith walk. Until a person reaches maturity they tend to look to externals for the answer to this question.

People look in a mirror to see what they look like on the outside. People look to those around them to tell them what they look like on the inside. People often don't know what their true gifts and abilities are until someone tells them. They need others to "mirror" or reflect back to them so they can learn about themselves from what others see. Spiritual moms provide a mirror of truth in a world of distortion.

This is why encouragement is so important for the person in the Seed stage. Like the child who is learning to walk or ride a bike, they are always looking to their mom to see how they are doing. People need to hear, "You are doing great!" "So glad you came!" "Thanks for making the choice to be here." "You have a wonderful smile." "I appreciate your attitude."

Speaking encouragement into a person's life is like water to the dry ground. Spiritual moms provide a mirror so people can see how their souls are doing and how their spirits are growing. Spiritual moms help tell people who they are in Christ.

Help Them Find the Answers. One of the ways that spiritual moms love is in helping people grow through finding the right answers themselves. Marge Caldwell shares, "My goal to is to get them started in the Word of God. I point them to the Bible and get the Scripture in them. It is important that young Christians start memorizing Scripture and plant the Word in their heart. I pray for them daily.

"The best thing one of the girls can say to me is 'I feel safe with you.' That's exactly what I should be—a safe harbor. People are looking for someone who is supportive and not looking towards them with criticism."

Praise and Nurture. Kaye Green believes in the importance of nurturing. "It is important to praise and encourage the growth that you see. Praise the Lord for them and what God is doing in their lives. Let them know that they are awesome and you are excited for them."

Acceptance. Anita Carson shares, "Some people have never had a mother who has embraced them. Sometimes I pat them on the head and run a hand through their hair. Some have been so wounded. Once a wounded individual gets a mother's acceptance it starts a healing process. This healing then leads them to a place where they can hear the Father's voice and receive His love."

Aunts Can Be Spiritual Moms, Too!

Misty is a spiritual mom to her nieces and nephews. Since the time they were babies, she has been dedicated to telling them about Jesus and building their faith in any way she can.

Aunts can minister to kids. I write them and tell them that they are very special and that I'm so glad that God put them in my family. I tell them that all the time so that they know that I mean it and will never forget it.

I send them e-mails and e-cards (which they love), call them on the phone, send them notes and stickers. I teach them to pray. Every time I am with them I try to teach them a spiritual lesson and plant God seeds inside of them.

For instance if we find money on the ground, I ask them

what we should do. I ask them what they think, even if they are just 4 years old. I am always surprised and blessed by the great answers. I want them to know that they are loved and to think like Jesus would want them to think.

Bless 'Em

God wants to bless people. The Bible says that the entire world would be blessed through the seed of Abraham. We are to be God's instruments of blessing in this world. After all, it is kindness that leads people to repentance. Romans 2:4 says that the goodness of God leads you to repentance. When people experience the unconditional love of God coming through others, they are blessed. When people receive an unexpected gift, hug, phone call, check in the mail, or meal, they are blessed. Blessings help melt the hardest hearts and heal those who think they have been forgotten.

Blessing others is a creative act of love. There are more ways to bless people than there are stars in the sky, yet God's people are always finding both new and old ways to bless people. Here are a few examples, both familiar and foreign.

Casserole Queen. My great-aunt, Virginia Campbell, or "Juju" to the children, was the Casserole Queen for Merion Presbyterian Church outside Philadelphia well into her early nineties. Even during the depression she was always there with a meal for a family or batch of cookies for the Sunday coffee. The church cookbooks made sure that her favorite recipes were prominently listed. She still remembers which casseroles were different ministers' favorites. Aunt Juju throughout her life was tirelessly positive and loved learning. She attended Sunday school class faithfully until she had to stop driving at age 92. At her hundredth birthday party, dozens of people from the church came to celebrate Aunt Juju's faith-filled life and to thank her for all the blessings and countless meals, desserts, and goodies that she had given in love.

Single moms need blessings, too! Single moms are a great ministry opportunity for churches. With the rising divorce rate and economic challenges, single moms are going through more traumatic things today than ten years ago. Childcare, groceries, car repair, basic home repair, and clothing are simple but critical needs that single moms have.

Debbie, a single mom with four children, shares, "The last six years have been so difficult. One of the biggest helps to me would have been if someone would have just come and taken the kids for a day. It would have blessed me for someone to come over and say, Here, take a break. Go shopping, take a nap, have some time to yourself. And spending time with my kids would have given them a perfect opportunity to speak into their lives and minister to them. The people that did help were the ones who really had no time to spare. When they did it really blessed me."

Tutoring touch. In the Asian culture, education is extremely important. Robin Watson and her husband work as missionaries in Taiwan and also teach at a private school. One of the most effective ways that Robin has found to reach the parents is to offer free tutoring.

In Taiwan, students have tremendous pressure to succeed because there is a limited number of schools and colleges. Good parents give their child an education and a good son or daughter sacrifices himself or herself by working hard. A typical 5th grader will meet with a tutor every night of the week for 2 hours, then come home and study two more hours. If it's time for tests then they will stay up later. All kids go to tutors on Saturdays.

Robin says that around 9th grade, the kids start to flip out and get into drugs or gangs. "The pressure is too great," she says, "and they think, No way am I smart enough to make it into the one high school in the city." Some students will go to a cram school for a whole year and if they don't make it into the one high school in the city, their parents have lost face, not to mention money.

"The biggest request that we get from parents and students is to pray when they have tests," Robin says. "We also found that by offering free English tutoring for their kids, parents who refuse to let a student come to church become more open to the gospel. When the parents realize that you are blessing their children and them by giving them something they would normally have to pay for, it makes them very receptive to the gospel."

Card ladies. Many churches have designated "card ladies" who bless people with greeting cards on important occasions, but in this electronic age this is becoming rare. Kaye Green shares, "I go through two or three boxes of cards a month. I send cards for birthdays, holidays, loss of a loved one, and thank you notes. People need to see something tangible, and a card is a great way to show them that they are loved and remembered."

Little things mean a lot. Some women need mothering in very basic ways. Many women haven't been taught some of the basic skills that our mothers taught us. They need to be taught practical things like how to clean a house, organize, cook, nurture their children, and just get it together.

Loving in crisis. People need to have someone there when they are going into surgery, especially those without immediate family nearby. A quick visit to the hospital is a blessing, and prayers in those times may seem simple to us, but they have more impact than we will ever know. When there is a death in the family, people need help in the simplest ways. Bringing something simple like a tray of luncheon meat, a loaf of banana bread, or a casserole helps nurture and comfort people in stressful times.

Extreme blessings. There is a church in Africa that believes that when a person becomes a Christian they should be given an example of what forgiveness means. After a person completes the membership classes, they are asked for a list of all their financial debt. The church pays the debt and sets them free from financial bondage. What a great way to bless people into the Kingdom!

People love surprises. God has such blessings stored up for us in Heaven, but He wants to bless us today, tomorrow, and forever. Spiritual moms are one of the real blessings in the world today. From leading in the prayer of salvation to having a cup of coffee, spiritual moms are always finding new ways to love people and nurture the seed of the gospel.

Macy Domingo: Blessing the Forgotten

Macy Domingo is considered the Oprah Winfrey of Africa. She was the creator and host of *Africa Life*, which was the first variety show produced and syndicated to the entire continent of Africa. Macy was famous and spent time with the political and entertainment leaders of nations in West Africa and Europe. After ten years of success, she ended the show to pursue other options. She had become a Christian and started a radio show called *Testimonies*, which shared the stories of answered prayer. Macy shares this story:

> One night around 2:00 in the morning, I was reading the mail from my listeners. It was very late and I opened this envelope from a Muslim in another country. I read,

My Dear Mother,

You will be surprised to read "my dear mother." I was born again through your radio show. I am a college student who is in the Douake prison. But since I gave my life to Christ my family abandoned me and refuses to help me. I can't listen to your radio program any more because I don't have any batteries for my radio. So I am very sad that I won't be able to listen to you any more. Your radio program has given me such hope and taught me about Jesus. I thank you for your show and hope that you remember me.

Your son in prison

As I read the letter, all I could do was weep.

The next day I called the prison and asked to speak to the prisoner. The prison guard was shocked and asked, "Are you really Macy Domingo?" I said yes. He said, "I will ask if you can talk to him."

Several minutes later they put the young man, Adama, on the phone. I told him, "I want you to know that because of Jesus you can have hope. Adama, I am the one you wrote to. This is Macy and I am so happy that you gave your life to Christ." He was crying over the phone and I assured him that by God's grace and help, I would find someone to send batteries, soap, and food.

Douake was one of the worst of the high security prisons in Cote d'Ivoire. The prisons are very primitive and prisoners depend upon families to bring them food, medical supplies and other necessities. What was strange was why Adama had been sent to a prison with violent criminals, when he had only been arrested for fighting with another college student.

God reminded me of the Scriptures, "When I was hungry you fed me, when I was thirsty you gave me drink, when I was in prison you came and visited me." Instead of sending someone I went to visit the prison myself. When I arrived the entire prison, Christians and Muslims, greeted me. For the next two years I would go and take tapes, cassettes, books, Bibles, and other things

Adama became an evangelist in prison, started Bible studies, organized prayer and cell groups, and taught other prisoners how to read. I would greet them from the radio and we would have prayer meetings to intercede for the work in the prison. In less than two years the number of Christians in the prison grew from dozens, to 400, to 800 salvations.

Once when I was visiting, a prisoner without a hand proudly brought me some wildflowers in a yogurt container. He had a wonderful smile on his face and was so happy to be able to present me with these simple flowers. I was so touched that I wanted to melt.

Later I got a letter from the growing prison family, "My Dear Mother, How can we imagine that someone like you would come to see us? We have been forgotten. We can't believe that you come to a place that is like hell. What you come and bring to us is too great. Thank you." All I could do was cry, humbled by their gratitude and wishing for millions of dollars to do more.

Chapter Six

The Feed Season: Strengthen the Gospel's Hold

Every brand-new baby born into this world is born looking for food, searching for the best nourishment that they innately know will sustain them. Once children taste the best food, they are ruined for anything less! As I viewed the wonder of my newborn baby eager to be fed and my sense of fulfillment from feeding her only food that is full of nutrients needed to keep her delicate new being healthy and satisfied, I understood more clearly my mission to help babes in Christ taste the goodness of God and to see them saturated in His manifest presence.
—Darlene Zschech, *Extravagant Worship*

In the '80s when the Information Age began to whirl forward, a sitcom about a neighborhood pub was an overnight success. *Cheers* touched the core need of Americans and people everywhere. Technology, satellites, and computers were changing all of our lives, whether we liked it or not. The speed of information was picking up more momentum than an Oklahoma twister. Families were busting up like cellophane wrappers, and morality was melting like crushed ice in a fast food cup. The Information Revolution was shaking everything from work to romance. The upheaval couldn't be stopped, but people were doing their best to ride the waves into the future.

With all this change, it's no wonder that *Cheers* became one of America's favorite sitcoms. The *Cheers* theme song was a clear reflection of the heart cry of millions.

Sometimes you want to go
Where everybody knows your name
And they're always glad you came.
You want to go where you can see,
Your troubles are all the same,
You want to go where everybody knows your name.

All of us need a safe place, a family, a place where we are truly loved and truly known. We were made for community and community was made for us. People are lonely. We know that in God's family people will find a place of peace and love. Spiritual moms help people to enter into God's family by inviting them into their homes and hearts.

The Feed season is the time in a Christian's faith walk when they are starting to grow in understanding and are learning how to feed themselves and walk on their own. A believer is beyond the salvation threshold and beginning to grow in godly understanding, wisdom, and knowledge. Lots of spiritual feeding and emotional tending and healing are required at this stage. It is also a time of building relationships. Spiritual moms help people learn what to feed their souls and spirits. Author Catherine Marshall explains:

The food we eat provides the building blocks out of which the tissues of our body are made. In the same way, what we "eat" via our thought and imaginative life provides the building blocks out of which our souls and spirits are built. They

are either nourished and grow in the knowledge and love of God, or else they atrophy and die. God means for us to look at the good, the beautiful, the true, the pure.
—Catherine Marshall, *Light in My Darkest Hour*

Feeding is done with the Word and worship. Large doses of Scripture will help people to feed their spirits, heal wounded hearts, cut free from destructive behavior patterns, and renew their minds. We tend to their needs through love, time, listening, counseling, and fellowship activities. Personal relationships help people to feel safe and loved so they have the courage to grow and change. Community relationships help people to feel connected and needed.

In the Feed season of a Christian's walk, spiritual moms help in the following ways:
- **Teach 'em**
- **Tend 'em**
- **Mend 'em**
- **Befriend 'em**

Teach 'Em

My son, keep your father's commands
and do not forsake your mother's teaching.
Bind them upon your heart forever;
fasten them around your neck.
When you walk, they will guide you;
when you sleep, they will watch over you;
when you awake, they will speak to you.
—Proverbs 6:20–22 NIV

Jesus was a teacher, and teacher was the first title He allowed people to call Him. Teaching was the main recorded activity of Jesus' ministry. Whether He was at the beach or in the temple, Jesus was always teaching through stories and parables. Jesus was often throwing out parables that seemed more like riddles. He would ask questions and not give the answers. Time after time the disciples would ask Him what things meant. In our modern world with multiple-choice answers, this teaching style would seem simplistic and baffling. Jesus' teaching style required that people listen with their hearts and spirits.

The Hebrew word for *teach* means to throw, shoot, cast, or pour like rain. This is what a true teacher does. They throw wisdom at us to see if we can catch the true meaning. They shoot out truth like arrows, hoping they hit the mark. They cast knowledge into our minds like a fisherman. They pour information into our lives, hoping that we can contain it.

Spiritual moms are teachers. They teach with their words and their lives. There is no limit to their lessons. They can teach anywhere, anytime, and on anything. What do they teach? They teach people how to build their walk of faith. They teach people how to live, love, walk, talk, serve, pray, tithe. They teach most everything that is necessary for the equipping of the saints to the building of the body of Christ.

> To prepare God's people for the works of service, so that the body of Christ may be built up until we all reach unity in the faith and in the knowledge of the Son of God and become mature, attaining to the whole measure of the fullness of Christ.
> —Ephesians 4:12–13 NIV

Begin with the Basics

Andrea Taylor asked her spiritual mom, Maxine, to disciple her when she was a young wife in 1983. Andrea and her sister-in-law met with Maxine once a week to do a Bible study together. Andrea relates:

> The first thing that Maxine taught me was how to become a godly wife and mother. She made me accountable with my home, housework, and dishes. For example, I didn't always make the bed in the morning, and she started calling me and asking me if I had gotten things done. After I got those things accomplished, we worked on attitudes and controlling my tongue.
>
> For example, I use to call my husband cheap. She helped me to restructure my thinking so that I called him frugal. I had to learn how to build my husband and family up instead of tearing them down with my words.
>
> Maxine had me come to events and asked me to help. One time she put me by the iced tea glasses and told me to pour for people. I remember when she asked me it seemed silly because people were perfectly capable of pouring their own drinks. But I did what she told me. Later I realized that she was teaching me how to serve people.

Give Practical Advice

Spiritual moms know that when they give practical advice, things will get done. It is important that people develop basic devotional and Bible study habits. Even if it is only ten or fifteen minutes at a time, they need to start. They need to learn how to feed themselves through Scripture memorization, listening to worship music or tapes, or getting involved in a study group. Even if a person doesn't have much time, spiritual moms can provide great suggestions on how to get started and maximize their time.

One of my spiritual moms, Anne Barge, taught me how important it is to fill your home with peace and godly music. When you walked into Anne's house, she always had worship or classical music on, which made you relax and leave the troubles of the day behind. I started doing the same thing when I was traveling as a consultant. Anne taught me when I came into a hotel room to pray and invite the Holy Spirit to fill the room where I was staying. Then I would play either music or teaching tapes in the evening and morning, as I was getting ready for work. Learning to change the "spiritual atmosphere" in the hotel room helped me to do a better job when I was consulting with television stations around the U.S.

Bring Them Alongside

Another important way for spiritual moms to feed and tend is to bring others alongside. This means finding ways to involve people in your everyday life or the life of the church. This provides many opportunities for becoming friends, for hearing needs, for making someone at home. Kaye Green shares:

> The best way to teach is by bringing someone alongside of me. I tell them, "Hey, I am going to do this, would you like to help?" You have to train them how to get ready for a meeting for thirty, set the table, and decorate and how to make coffee. You just can't give them a list and assume that they know how to organize and execute something. It's important that you work together and explain why you are doing things in a certain manner.
>
> Years ago I learned a great lesson. We were having a Christmas party and I had given this young woman several things to do. The day of the Christmas party she called and said she was not coming. I said, Wait a second; you are in charge of x, y, z for the party. She said, I can't come; I am going to a movie with my daughter. I found out later that she didn't know how to do what she had volunteered for and was too embarrassed to ask for help. I have now learned to ask people if they have ever done this before. Never assume people know how to do something.

Tend 'Em

Tend means to minister to the needs of, to look after, to take care of, to serve, to wait upon. *Tend* is the root of the word *tender*. Jesus described Himself as the good shepherd. From pasture to bandages, a good shepherd knows how to attend to the needs of his flock. I think of "tending" as something that we do to strengthen a person's emotion and will.

Encouragement is a great way to tend the sheep. When church counselor and spiritual mom Marge Caldwell meets with people, here is what she does: "Toward the end of a counseling session before we pray together I ask people an important question. Do you know why God has allowed us to have this time together? They usually say no. I tell them, it is to allow you to be used by God for someone else. Nothing goes to waste with the Lord. Every experience you have been through He intends for you to use to help someone else."

Robin Watson and her family have been in the mission field since 1986. They were stationed in China until the Tiananmen Square incident of 1989, but then they moved to Taiwan. Robin works in a private school while her husband pastors an English-speaking church in the third largest city in Taiwan. As a teacher and pastor's wife in Taiwan, Robin finds herself fulfilling the needs of several groups: the families of students, the children of the missionaries, and young Chinese women. She says:

The Chinese people first touched me because everyone was so sad. When you get to know them, they had lived such a sad life. When we first moved to China, we talked to a man who had been an academic. After the revolution he was forced to work as a street cleaner and denied a food rationing card. He had survived by eating grass. It is a very difficult life because people are told where they can work. Young couples are told when they can get married, have a child, and where to live. Many families are separated by an entire continent and only able to see their family twice a year during the two official vacations.

When we first lived in China we had to be very careful of relationships. There is such a prejudice against foreigners that one young man, who had helped us with simple tasks such as grocery shopping, told us his whole family had been punished for being friends with foreigners.

In the school we have many children of the missionaries who are paying a high cost for being in the field with their parents. Missionaries know that their children are the main reason they return from the field. It is always stressful and hard on the kids, especially when the dad is away on the mission field. We try to help cover for the parents when they are out and say, "We have your kids covered."

One family had a series of challenges with their preteen son, who was experiencing a great deal of stress when his dad and sometimes mom were gone for up to a month at a time. The family was under a great deal of spiritual attack every time the dad left; once the house nearly burnt down, and then there was an earthquake. The boy was having problems in school, with discipline, and was suicidal. I started tutoring him and helping him deal with his classes one at a time. Now he is a well-adjusted 8th grader and is off the anti-depressants and making good grades.

Mend 'Em

You are walking through a mall or are shopping at a department store, and as you look around that rack of clothes you see an active 4-year-old who has run off when his mother's back was turned. We have seen the face that a child makes when he doesn't see his mother, as he goes from wide-eyed search, to panic, to hysterical crying. It doesn't matter what you say, or how you try to help, nothing will calm the frightened child until he is once again safe in the arms of his mother.

There is nothing like the comfort of a mom's arms wrapped around you. As babies, we first experience love in our mother's arms. Newborns need to be held in order to feel safe, protected, and loved. It is not good for any of us to be alone; we were made to be in relationship and community.

Too many people are starving for touch and relationship. Visit an orphanage in a Third World nation and it will change your life—that is, as soon as you stop crying. Imagine dozens of beautiful children begging for you to simply hold them. But remember, you don't have to go overseas to discover how popular your lap can be. Try spending lunch at a daycare; you will be amazed how popular you will be. And if babies aren't your speed, go visit a local nursing home and talk to folks who have a great story to share. There is a definite premium on individual attention for the preschool crowd or at a nursing home.

Healing Counsel

Spiritual moms are excellent counselors. Spiritual moms help heal the hearts and lives of others. They help people heal by listening, praying, counseling, as well as teaching people to apply forgiveness, grace, and mercy to the wounds of the past. Some spiritual moms are professional counselors; others are just using their God-given gifts to serve others. It is important that people are healed so that the pain of the past doesn't destroy the joy of the future.

For my life, the Lord knew what He was doing when he gave me Annie Barge as a spiritual mom. She has several degrees, including a master's in counseling, and is a licensed therapist and teacher. Throughout the years Annie's advice has been like gold to me. As a fellow teacher she was always there to help guide me. She was a trusted counselor who would listen when I talked, and would honestly point out my errors.

But Annie wasn't the only one who blessed me; there was Joan, Nancy, Fell, Louise, Barbara, Sandy, Naomi, Juju, and many, many more. Some of the best times of my life have been spending a evening or weekend with one of these fabulous women, propped up between pillows, sipping a cup of tea—laughing, talking, crying, and sharing the night away.

Marge Caldwell is a church counselor, teacher, and spiritual mom to hundreds in Houston. Here is one exercise she uses to help people heal with making a gifts and talents assessment.

When I am counseling with someone I start with where they are emotionally, spiritually, mentally, and physically. After they have revealed their heart and see what their problems are then I take them back to the Bible. If I am dealing with a person with poor self-esteem, I will have them take a piece of paper with four columns on it. At the top of each column is one of four categories: physical, mental, emotional, spiritual. I make them write up what they like best about themselves in each of these areas. I don't let them list anything negative—only personal assets. This allows them to brag on God and focus on the positive.

Befriend 'Em

Being a friend to people is one of the most healing things that can be done, especially for women. Research proves how important this is to a person's physical and emotional well being. There are lots of ways to befriend people. Churches are always providing opportunities for people to make friends. Some women are able to find a spiritual mom at church or through activities. At First Baptist in Houston, they have found several ways to help women find spiritual guidance and mentoring. In addition to numerous Bible studies and exercise classes, the women's missions department has developed two other programs, First Place and Sisters of Influence.

First Place was developed in 1984 as a way to help women lose weight and get in shape from a biblical perspective. Since then over a half a million women across the world have come and renewed their lives and bodies through the First Place program. Carol Lewis, director of the program, shares, "My ministry is to hurting women. Most of the women will tell you that losing weight is a wonderful by-product of First Place. We help women grow in four areas—spiritually, mentally, emotionally, and physically."

It's All About Obedience

The website is filled with hundreds of testimonies of how women became healthy on the inside and out. They are healed first in their spirit and then built up so they can make permanent change in their eating habits and personal behaviors. One of the reasons why it works is that women form relationships and support structure for lifelong health.

"Anyone can buy the program and start a group. The participants love seeing the leader losing weight with them," explains Carol. "First Place has a much better success rate than the national average (25% versus 5%). I believe that the secret is that we teach people to believe, trust, and obey God. You can read all the diet books you want but if a person doesn't obey God it won't do them any good. As I was writing my last book, the Lord reminded me of John 14:21: 'Whoever has my commands and obeys them, he is the one who loves me. He who loves me will be loved by my Father, and I too will love him and show myself to him.'"

Carol continues, "This is where real success is found. If children will obey there is nothing a parent won't do for them; how much more God wants to give His children." Spiritual moms help to lead others into loving obedience so that they will see God more clearly.

Sisters of Influence

Church-based mentoring programs are a great way to connect spiritual orphans and those who need guidance with a spiritual mom. Carolyn O'Neal, director of women's missions at First Baptist Church in Houston, describes how they started their program, Sisters of Influence. She shares:

I had a desire for women to come alongside of each other because so much is learned at the feet of wise women. One of our members, Dena Lee, is an executive with an oil company. She had a passion to see women mentored in a godly way, so we worked together and developed Sisters of Influence.

We didn't want to use the word mentors because it scares the older women away, because they think, "I can't mentor; what do I know?" We put announcements in the bulletins asking young women if they would like someone to help them with their walk. We also began asking mature women if they would consider being a mentor for a younger woman. We designed a personality profile and then began the matching. From each pair of women, we asked for a one-year commitment, which is to be taken very seriously. We launched with a lunch, and Marge Caldwell, who is a major spiritual mom in the house, did a commissioning for the women.

This was a real spiritual journey for us all, but we are seeing such results! We found books for both the women and mentorees to read to help develop guidelines. Dena taught the group some basics of what to expect and then one of the counselors helped teach about dos and don'ts. We tried to give balance to the mentors to protect them. If a person had deeper emotional issues that needed work with a professional counselor, we taught them how to recognize the difference.

We suggested that the women set the framework for their relationship: some meet once a week, others monthly, some for dinner, others for Bible studies. We did not put restrictions but let each couple shape what works best for them. Many of them are still meeting and now some of the younger women are becoming mentors themselves.

Most of the couples really clicked. Clarice was in her 70s and Lindsey was in her 20s, but even though Lindsey has a godly mother, she grew a tremendous amount with Clarice. This year, Lindsey is going to teach the other new recruits how to get the most out of this opportunity.

Bridging to a New Life

"One of the great success stories for Sisters of Influence was Susan (not her real name), a young woman who had a problem with alcohol, had given up a child for adoption, and was trying to restart her life by attending graduate school in Houston. I was able to partner Susan with an older woman who had gone through part of the same journey. They became the dearest of friends. Even though Susan has completed graduate school and moved away, she still keeps in touch with her mentor and friends at First Baptist. We are all so proud of how she is doing and is making great strides in her career and spiritual walk. Susan, like many of the young women, tells us that having someone to help guide them in a godly direction changed their lives," says Carolyn O'Neal.

Just as it is difficult to count the number of apples on a tree, it is difficult to count the spiritual fruit of a spiritual mom. Her children are many and they keep multiplying in new and exciting ways.

I tell you the truth, anyone who has faith in me will do what

I have been doing. He will do even greater things than these, because I am going to the Father.
—John 14:12 NIV

Jesus said that we would do greater things than He did. This is hard to imagine, but then I consider the "fresh bread" that spiritual moms are serving to the multitudes, and then it seems to make sense.

∽

Marge Caldwell: Spiritual Mom of Spiritual Moms

Spiritual moms often work behind the scenes loving, listening, and helping to launch others. Marge Caldwell at First Baptist Church in Houston is a spiritual mother at this church and over the years has helped train and launch some significant women in ministry. Considering that she has been teaching and counseling at First Baptist for over 25 years, it is obvious that she and her husband are pillars in the house.

Carolyn O'Neal, Carol Lewis, and many other women credit Marge with being one of the reasons they are able to do what they do today. She is a wonderful example, teacher, and friend. Carolyn shares:

Marge is everything that we as women want to be. She is godly, she is wise, she is beautiful, and she is funny. She loves unconditionally. She will often just call me up and say, Carolyn I just LOOOOOVVVVVVE you and you are doing such an incredible job.

Marge is 89 years young. When she speaks to any of our women's groups, old or young, they are eating out of her hand. She isn't afraid to tell funny stories about herself like climbing over a bathroom stall to surprise someone and discovering that she surprised the wrong person. Her husband Chuck is her biggest fan.

One of the reasons Marge is successful is that she is always challenging and pushing people to do something for God. They all respond…"Oh not me. God couldn't use me! I am such a mess." Marge reminds them that, "You sound just like Peter. Remember that he only had a 6th grade education, was bad-tempered and explosive, and God used him. Why couldn't God use you?"

Marge tells about one young woman she met about fifteen years ago who was teaching some aerobics classes at the church. During a couple of counseling sessions, this attractive young mother told Marge, "I hope that God can use me a little like He does you." She expressed an interest in teaching, and Marge started giving her some pointers on how to teach, organize a lesson, and speak in public.

Several years later as Marge was organizing the annual women's retreat, she met with this same young woman and asked her if she would be willing to teach the early morning aerobics class as she had done in previous years. This year the young woman asked Marge if she could teach a session. Marge asked her what she was going to talk about. She replied: "Jesus. I want to talk about Jesus."

Marge said yes and realized that normally she never let anyone teach a class unless she had first watched or heard them teach elsewhere. Marge hoped that she had made the right decision trusting this beginner. During the retreat she happened to stop in the back of the room during this first timer's session and was amazed. The room was packed with women who were hanging on every word that the young woman shared. "It was wonderful. She was a natural teacher." Everyone was thrilled, and that was Beth Moore's first official class at First Baptist.

A short time later Chuck, Marge's husband, had to go in the hospital and Marge asked Beth if she would cover for her and teach five classes. The young mother agreed. Later when Marge called the leaders to see how she had done, those who had been cautious, saying, "Who is she?" were now saying, "Beth Moore—where has she been all these years?"

And birthed by the trust of a spiritual mom, Beth Moore's Bible teaching career began. The crowds at her weekly Bible study are between 2,000–3,000, and millions of women have been blessed by her speaking ministry, her Bible studies, her videos, and her books.

In the years that followed, Marge and Beth have become very close friends. Several years ago, after Beth's mother passed away, she asked Marge if she would become her surrogate mother. Marge, whose own daughter had passed away from cancer more than ten years previously, said yes. Marge and Beth meet for lunch every few weeks. Marge is always there to listen, counsel, pray, encourage. Marge shares, "Like all of us, Beth needs a safe place where she can get things off her chest and receive godly counsel. We all need someone—with skin on—that we can talk to. Chuck and I pray constantly for Beth and her family. We are so proud of Beth and how God is using her."

Beth adds, "No one has impacted my adult life and ministry more than Marge Caldwell. Her unconditional love, sound counsel, and unwavering support have spanned two decades. I will never understand the grace of God to grant me favor with such a woman of God. I am mad about Marge."

Chapter Seven

The Weed Season: Pruning Away Hindrances

We have to learn that the single most important element in any human relationship is real honesty—with oneself, with God, and with others, what Jesus called 'Walking in the light.' Admit it, we parents make mistakes in judgment, understanding, and behavior. There are times we need to ask forgiveness of our children. In doing so, we build a bridge of relationship over which love can travel.
—Catherine Marshall, in *Guideposts*

Before we can make God real to someone else, He has to be real to us. As spiritual moms, we need to monitor the growth of those in our care to see where they are in their walk. After they move through the seeding and feeding stages, it is time for the weeding and pruning stage. This is the time when we look at the conditions of spiritual gardens and test the fruit.

"Son-Ripened" and Vine Nourished

I love homegrown tomatoes. There is nothing quite like a summertime Beefsteak tomato sandwich on homemade wheat bread. Growing up in Bethesda, Maryland, meant that, at the crack of dawn on Saturdays, Farmer's Market was the first stop on the errand list. In the summer, we would buy homemade bread and sweet rolls and baskets of summer squash and would carefully choose a basket of beautiful, firm tomatoes. In our house my dad was the sandwich chef. Dad would take all of his engineering expertise and carefully slice the tomatoes and strategically arrange the pieces of tomato so that each sandwich bite had the same amount of juicy "yummy-ness."

Nowadays, getting to the farmer's market is a rare occasion, so I have to buy my tomatoes at the grocery store...and I am usually disappointed. I have tried different shapes, sizes, and brands, but even though the tomatoes look great in the store, most of them don't have any flavor. These tomatoes are picked green, removed too early from the vine, and colored artificially, so they lack the flavor only the sun can provide.

What Flavor Is Your Faith?

This reminds me of the same problem Jesus had with the religious leaders and believers. Jesus challenges us all to be salt and light: *"You are the salt of the earth. But if the salt loses its saltiness, how can it be made salty again?...You are the light of the world."* (Matthew 5:13–14 NIV).

There are many who are like salt and tomatoes without flavor—people who look great on the outside but their lives have no flavor. Jesus warns us all not to be like the Pharisees and Sadducees, who have a form and type of religion that looks great on the outside but is all show and no taste. More than 80% of people in America say they are Christians, yet how many people are really living their faith? Like tomatoes, people have been removed prematurely from the vine and have not had enough time in the sun, meaning that people are not staying connected to the Father (source of life) and not exposing themselves to the light and truth of the Son.

Cultivating Authenticity

God desires us to be fruitful. The fruit of our lives is meant to feed others. The question that each person needs to ask of herself is, "If a person were to take a bite of the fruit from my life, would she come back for more?"

Just as people are tired of tasteless tomatoes, people are tired of artificial Christians. They want the real stuff. And so does God. People want honesty, stuff that works—people who really love and are willing to set a standard for others to live by. People want real heroes they can look up to and values that are worth living and dying for.

One small homegrown tomato with flavor is better than a plateful of the pithy, tasteless variety. Authenticity takes time to develop, but it is worth the flavor that gives it life.

Season Three—Weed and Prune

This is the "growing up season," which is sometimes painful but is worth the struggle. Spiritual moms are very important in the Weed and Prune season of a person's growth. They challenge, they confront, they help pull things out of people's lives, and they help pull them back in the boat when they are drowning.

Embracing discipline, dying to self, and crucifying the flesh are never anyone's favorite spiritual activities. But love calls, faith answers, and maturity responds. Weeding begins with learning how to control ungodly thoughts, words, and actions that come from within. Weeding is something that we must do with our own hands. When we repent of our actions we choose to remove the sin and unrighteousness out of our lives. Spiritual moms help us to weed our lives by helping us recognize the sin. Faithful are the wounds of a spiritual mother that point out the spiritual disease in our lives and hearts.

Pruning begins when we learn to react in a godly manner to difficult people and circumstances and learn to choose God's will over our own. In the pruning stage it is God's hand, not our own, that brings the lesson. Spiritual moms model these principles by teaching, leading, and setting personal examples in times of trial and difficulty.

Here are several additional points to remember about this critical season:

1. Weeding is for taking things out of our lives. Weeds steal nutrients from the soil, choke the plants, and crowd out the crop. In the parable of the four soils (Mark 4:1–20 and Matthew 13:1–23), the seed in the third group fell among the weeds and tares, and the weeds choked the plants and destroyed their fruitfulness. Jesus reminded us that the enemy would try to sow tares or weeds into the fields of our lives. Weeding must be done in order for the plants to survive. Behaviors such as envy, cheating, lying, gossip, and procrastination all steal our energy and are destructive to the lives of those around us. This is the time when the tares that have been planted in their lives may be thriving and need to be uprooted to protect the fruit.

2. Pruning develops greater fruitfulness: self-discipline, obedience, and character (John 15). When God prunes our lives and keeps us from going in a certain direction or following a certain career or relationship, it is to help keep us on His paths of greater fruitfulness. The hard part is recognizing this, but I recommend the book *In His Face* by Bob Sorge to help you identify the pruning hand of God.

3. Strength is built from resistance. Like muscles, character doesn't develop on its own. It requires some heavy lifting, practice, and resistance training to develop. Like Naomi experienced in the foreign land, the valleys of pain and bitterness help fortify our faith and change the lives of others. Challenging and exhorting others to develop godly character is the job of spiritual parents.

4. Timing is critical. It is easier to weed my garden when the soil is moist and loosely packed. It is easier to weed things out of people's hearts when they have been saturated with the Word, prayer, worship, and are in a digging mode. When you take behaviors and things out of a person's life, be ready to fill in the spaces with fellowship, memorizing the Word, Bible study, prayer, and fellowship.

Spiritual moms love to work in God's garden. They are great fruit inspectors and are always there with words that set us free from the sin that entangles us or encourage us to finish the race. Whether they are in person or speaking from a book, spiritual moms know that their own lives provide the greatest plumb line for others. The spiritual mom whose story you are about to read challenged millions to dream bigger.

Catherine Marshall: Dream Bigger
Catherine Marshall was a spiritual mom who through her writing challenged millions to embrace Christ and walk in greater knowledge of God. Catherine was able to do this because she was honest and taught others about the ways that God and circumstances were always weeding and pruning her life, heart, and spirit.

Certain books are so well known and make such an impact that they create a powerful message in our culture. Books like *Little Women*, *Catch-22*, and *To Kill a Mockingbird* make an indelible impression and change your life. Catherine Marshall's book *Christy* was one of those books for me, and probably for many of you. I read *Christy* years ago in high school and later heard about the story from Ken Wales, an award-winning film producer who after years of struggle produced the wonderful *Christy* television series. But until a friend mentioned Catherine Marshall and I began reading her old *Guideposts* articles, I really wasn't aware of how remarkable her accomplishments are and the magnitude of the impact she has made as a spiritual mother.

A Naomi of Today

Catherine's life reminded me of the biblical Naomi—it was filled with unexpected adversity and hardships. Her struggles with widowhood, single parenting, abandonment, fear, stepchildren, and depression speak to women today. Yet Catherine turned the bitterness of life into beauty through writing. Her many books and articles had a remarkable transparency, and her testimony of triumph became a beacon of light to others.

The public response to her writing was nothing less than remarkable. Catherine wrote or edited nearly twenty books and sold over eighteen million. She had five bestsellers, including *Christy*, which later became a television show. Catherine was a frequent contributor to *Guideposts* magazine, which is read by millions. Looking at such success, we don't see what the road was like getting there. We may see the mountains on the horizon but not realize that the road to the high places was rocky, treacherous, costly, and filled with detours. It is difficult to measure the cost of the struggles to reach the high places.

Catherine inherited a gift for ministry from both parents. Her father was a preacher and her mother was the original Christy, a missionary teacher in the backwoods of Tennessee. Catherine met her husband while attending college in Atlanta. Peter Marshall was an energetic and dynamic preacher from Scotland who became the chaplain to the U.S. Senate. Peter died prematurely of a heart attack at the age of 47, leaving 34-year-old Catherine to raise their 9-year-old son.

Shortly afterwards she began writing two books: a book of Peter Marshall's sermons, *Mr. Jones, Meet the Master*, and his biography, *A Man Called Peter*. There were many who questioned her writing. Catherine shared in a *Guideposts* article, "About midway in the manuscript, I received devastating criticism from one whose judgment I trusted....The realization of my inadequacy as a writer was not only an intellectual one. It was also emotional; there were plenty of tears. In my helplessness, there was no alternative but to put the project into God's hands."

The critics were wrong, and within three years both books were bestsellers and *A Man Called Peter* was optioned for a movie.

Truth Walking

Catherine's love for writing first served as her means of survival and then became her instrument of ministry. When Catherine began writing about the challenges she faced with widowhood, single parenting, and depression, the mindset of society was very different from the one we know today. In the '50s and '60s people didn't talk about these issues, much less write about them. There was a prejudice against psychologists; people felt only "crazy" people went to them. People simply stuffed the pain of life inside and ignored it. Catherine's writings did the opposite; they had remarkable openness, courage, and intensity. Catherine exposed her personal weeds and shared the pain of pruning with her readers. In another *Guideposts* article, she shares:

> In the period immediately following my husband's death, I felt that much of the structure of my life was gone....I found every road a dead end but one. My conclusion is that there is only one belonging in the universe on which we can finally depend—our belonging to Jesus Christ.
>
> There is an important truth for all of us about God's way of comforting. His is not the feather-cushion kind. He never commiserates with us, because that would nurture self-pity. Rather God comforts us with strength by adding resources...increasing one's "capacity for endurance." It makes us remember that the word "comfort" is derived from *fortis*, meaning "strength" or "strong." So God's comfort has steel in its backbone. It's a bugle call for reinforcements—which He supplies.

Readers embraced Catherine's honesty and transparency. "Catherine took her writing very seriously. I always respected the fact that she was more concerned about the quality than her ego," states bestselling author Elizabeth Sherrill, who was Catherine's book editor and friend.

"People would say to me, 'I would love to have known Catherine as you do,' but actually they did. Her readers were getting the real Catherine more than they would in person. Catherine was more of an introvert, but through her writing she was able to let out what was inside, which was a warm, loving, giving, and caring person that she really was. What she couldn't do in person she did through her writing."

Regardless of why or how Catherine came to write the way she did, her honesty shaped a unique literary voice that was decades ahead of its time and universal in its relevance.

The Father Knows Best

Catherine invited her readers to walk with her through all the hills and valleys of her faith walk. From widowhood, illness, depression, the challenges of being a single mom in a time when it was rare, to the joy of being remarried and the fear of becoming a stepmother to three young children, Catherine was a pioneer and voice that addressed the complex challenges facing women—juggling work and family, blending families, step-parenting, and ministry. Here she speaks of her stepdaughter:

> Occasionally I felt close to Linda; more often, like a rejected parent. I struggled with all the negative stepmother images. At times, I caught myself deeply resenting this youngster with all her attitudes....One Sunday in church I was thinking about Linda when suddenly in my mind and heart God's voice spoke to me with particular clarity and intensity. *Unless you love her, you don't love Me.*
>
> I well knew that resentments are emotions so deeply imbedded that we cannot shed them by wishing them away. And at that point I got a fresh view of the meaning of the Cross: our resurrected Lord stands before us, nail-pierced hand outstretched. "Hand me your resentments, your grudges, your anger. All of them."

All of her friends and family agreed that Catherine was a complex character. Dick Schneider, editor of *Guideposts*, worked with Catherine longer than any of her publishers. He relates: "Catherine Marshall revealed a new vision of the Christian faith and how to apply it personally—how to find comfort, direction, and hope. Catherine opened my eyes to the truth of it. She was able to take Scripture down to a level where you could understand what it means."

Calling the Question—Weeding for Truth

Catherine's personality and writings challenged everyone around her to move to the next level. She was able to directly ask or "call the question" that would help people get out of a rut and move to the next level.

"Catherine had a way of seeing into a person," Dick Schneider relates. "She would talk to a person and even if they wanted to talk about other things, she would see their problem and ask very direct questions about their issue. It didn't matter what the sin—gossip, lie, or lust. She could hone in on it and ask a direct question and get the person to open up about the issue."

Elizabeth and John Sherrill were close friends and coworkers at *Guideposts* with Catherine Marshall and her second husband, Leonard LeSourd. During their early years together, John was diagnosed with cancer. After the first round of operations the doctors discovered that John had a second lump and that immediate treatment was necessary. Elizabeth and John were devastated that John had to go back in for surgery immediately. Catherine and Len called and asked if they could come over before John went to the hospital.

Catherine boldly asked John if he truly believed Jesus was real. She kept probing and told him to release his pride. Later that evening, John received Jesus as Lord and experienced a miraculous healing.

Catherine Marshall and Diane Sawyer

Catherine's willingness to challenge herself increased her boldness and ability to "call the question" with others.

When we plant seeds for God, we never know what the harvest will be. As a teenager, the well-known television journalist Diane Sawyer had a very memorable encounter. She tells the story:

Many of us, I think, can look back and recall certain specific moments in our lives that take on greater importance the longer we live....For me, one of those moments occurred when I was 17 years old. I was a high school senior in Louisville, Kentucky, representing my state in the 1962 America's Junior Miss competition in Mobile, Alabama. Along with the other young contestants, I was doing my best to hold up under the grueling weeklong schedule of interviews, agonies over hair that curled or wouldn't, photo sessions, nervous jitters, and rehearsals. In the midst of it all, there was one person who stood at the center—at least my psychological center—someone I viewed as an island in an ocean of anxiety.

She was one of the judges. A well-known writer. A woman whose sea-gray eyes fixed on you with laser penetration, whose words were always deliberate. She felt the right words could make all the difference. Her name was Catherine Marshall.

From the first moment I met Catherine Marshall, I was aware that she was holding me—indeed all of us—to a more exacting standard. While other pageant judges asked questions about favorite hobbies and social pitfalls, she sought to challenge. She felt even 17-year-old girls—perhaps especially 17-year-old girls—should be made to examine their ambitions and relate them to their values.

During the rehearsal on the last day of the pageant, the afternoon before it would all end, several of us were waiting backstage when a pageant official said Catherine Marshall wanted to speak with us. We gathered around. Most of us were expecting a last-minute pep talk or the ritual good luck wish, or at most an exhortation to be good citizens, but we were surprised.

She fixed her eyes upon us. "You have set goals for your-selves. I have heard some of them. But I don't think you have set them high enough. You have talent and intelligence and a chance. I think you should take those goals and expand them. Think of the most you could do with your lives. Make what you do matter. Above all, dream big."

It was not so much an instruction as a dare. I felt stunned, like a small animal fixed on bright lights.

—Diane Sawyer, "Daring to Dream Big," in *Guideposts*, March 1986.

In the years to follow, Catherine and her husband Len LeSourd formed a strong friendship with Diane. Diane says that Catherine always told her to "dream bigger." And she did.

Using All Her Gifts

Len LeSourd, Catherine's second husband, said that he never knew of anyone, male or female, who used their God-given gifts to the full extent like Catherine. Len said that Catherine believed that people learned more from her mistakes than her successes, which is why she wrote about them.

After years of health challenges, Catherine Marshall died in 1983 at the age of 63. Catherine was not afraid to challenge those around her as she took up the cross in her own self-examination. Even though it has been twenty years since her passing, her life and writings are still bring-ing the gospel to light and making Jesus real to countless millions. Len shares, "Throughout her life, in every tough situation—the loss of her husband, the challenge of single parenting, the death of two grandchildren, the clash of strong wills in a household—Catherine turned to her Redeemer. Even when He seemed farthest away, in the darkness of her own rebellion and alienation, she clung to the simple fact of His existence—in the absence of all feeling or evidence."

Scripture tells us that the Lord sings over His children. When we arrive at heaven's gate I often imagine that as we enter into the presence of the Lord, the angels will sing a welcoming song of love—a testimony of God's goodness in our lives and the righteousness of Christ revealed.

Through the valleys of sorrows and past the mountains of difficulties that Catherine walked, you could always hear a pure melody of faith in her words. Each experience and sorrow added its own dimension to the song of Catherine's life until there was a symphony of great beauty and majestic proportions.

Through her writings, the struggles and victories in Catherine's life were shaped into a godly orchestration. What were once devastating crashes of disappointment were transformed into percussive exclamations of miraculous power. The hollow sounds of loneliness were caressed with prayer until the loving breath of heaven whispered peace. The plucking sounds of anxiety were dissolved with the washing, calming waves of rest. The fearful bugle of alarm harmoniously blended with dozens of heavenly trumpets proclaiming the holiness of the King.

With her life and writing, Catherine Marshall challenges us and the world to listen to the voice of heaven, walk the path of faith, and, when we look in the mirror, to dream bigger.

Do you have any rivers in your life that seem uncrossable, any mountains that you have not yet tunneled through? Take heart—these are the very adventures in which our God delights.
—Catherine Marshall, "Dare to Dream the Impossible," *Guideposts*, June 1963.

Chapter Eight

The Lead Season: Releasing to God's Call

God asks no man whether he will accept life.
That is not the choice. You must take it.
*The only choice is **how**.*
—Henry Ward Beecher, *Life Thoughts*

The fourth and final season of spiritual mothering is the Lead season, when a spiritual mom releases her child to fulfill God's call in her life. Spiritual moms are the touch point, the hug, the loving face, the kind word, the push out the door, the kick in the behind that launches people toward their destiny.

This final season is when spiritual moms both lead and release God's children into God's future. When we lead others we are also preparing for them to lead. Spiritual moms need to have understanding and vision so that they can cast a vision for those they have been leading. This is a time when spiritual moms can help turn the spotlight of truth on the future.

As result, new leaders are born, new paths are begun, and new lives are won. Through their guidance, training, and prayers, this is the time when spiritual moms give "flying lessons." Spiritual moms will lead their pupils to the edge of the cliff and encourage them to spread their wings of faith and leap off into the spiritual winds of opportunity.

Flying Lessons

So how do we teach people to fly? Let's observe an expert, the eagle. The mother eagle knows that both coaxing and discomfort motivate her little eaglets.

First, the mother eagle will coax the young birds to the edge of the nest by offering food from a distance. But when the time comes for the eaglets to begin flying on their own, the mother eagle has a new way to encourage her children to start to fly. The female eagle will start to tear out the lining of the nest and throw it away. What was once a warm, comfortable bed for the chicks, where food was dropped from the sky, is transformed into a very unpleasant bed of branches and sticks for the adolescent eagles.

You can imagine what the young eagles are thinking. "Doesn't mom realize that I am starving? Why are mom and dad keeping that big fat salmon all to themselves? Boy, it sure is drafty in this nest. Why in the world did mom have to start redecorating and tear apart a perfectly good nest? Hey, where are they going? You guys come back here! Don't leave me. I'm hungry! Oh well, I guess I better jump and go after them. Geronimo! Wow, these wings really do work after all."

A final point to remember is that the mother eagle is watching for the young birds to make that leap out of the nest. She stays close by, and if an eaglet flounders the mother will sweep underneath, catch them on her back, and take them to another perch so they can try again.

Here is what the eagle teaches us about leading and releasing:

• People must fly on their own, even though they don't want to. Let people discover what God has for them, even if it is clear to you. People have to go through the discipline of hearing and seeking God's will on their own; otherwise they will never finish the race.

• Encourage people to take small leaps of faith toward what God is calling them to do. The mother eagle let the eaglets build their confidence by balancing on the edge of the nest first. Don't force people to take steps of faith before they are ready for them. Give simple tasks like opening a meeting in prayer, leading the Bible study, supervising a compassion event. Working alongside someone teaches and builds confidence simultaneously.

• Give people a push out of the nest when it is time to fly. This what the mother eagle does when she tears apart the nest and makes the discomfort level of the babies greater than the fear of flying. Sometimes people don't realize that they are ready to do something and they need a spiritual mom to point the direction. Ask the Holy Spirit to direct you to both the right project and timing.

• Watch and help them through those first days of flying. Mother eagles are there to coach and catch their chicks. Be ready to help them work through their learning curve and early mistakes. Spiritual moms are ready to listen, counsel, bless, and support them with love for years after they have left the nest.

Making Sacrifices

The fourth season in the Christian life, the Lead and Release season, is about releasing those you have discipled and trained into leadership so they are able to accomplish their destiny and do what God has called them to do. This is the natural cycle of growth. Spiritual mothering is about helping push the next generation and all people into the call that God has for them. Spiritual parents are willing to sacrifice to make that happen—and serve what God is doing through them.

> Spiritual moms—they plow the ground. You don't do it for self, you do it for those who follow after you. It is the same for natural mothers who plow the ground for their children. You want them to be better and will sacrifice to help them be whatever they are called to be. It is the same for spiritual parents. I want my spiritual children to teach better than I do and go on more missions than I can.
> —Anita Carson

Help others launch! One of the most exciting and rewarding things that a spiritual parent can experience is when a person comes to them ripe with vision and prepared to launch a new mission or project that God has given them. It is so wonderful to see the Kingdom being multiplied in this manner.

> I love to teach and speak into the lives of pastors' wives and women in leadership. We were taught in seminary that the pastors should remain distant from the congregation and not become close friends. I don't agree with that belief, because how can we mentor people if they don't know who we are? Over the years, it has been our relationships and friendships that have literally birthed dozens of other pastors, churches, and ministries across the country and world.
> —Sybil Griffing, wife of Pastor Olen Griffing

Embrace differences. One of the important things spiritual moms remember is that just as every person is different, the way God works through people is also unique. Too often a great idea or program is crushed because the form, style, and methods may be uncomfortable to church leadership. Spiritual moms are important ambassadors for helping introduce people with new and fresh ideas into a church program. Spiritual moms help others to lead well and carry the plans to completion. God is creative, and we need to release people into all the creative paths that the Lord intends.

Passing the baton. There often comes a time when those who have been leading change places with those who are following. Spiritual moms look forward to the time when they can pass the baton on to the next wave of leadership. It is a wonderful thing to see others walking in victory and doing more than you ever dreamed possible.

Servant leader. Leading is much more than giving orders; it is about inspiring, directing, sacrificing, and caring for the needs of others. When we are teaching others to lead it is important that we remember that God gives a different model for leadership than the world. True leaders in God's eyes are those who have the heart of a servant. This model requires Christlike character and spirit-filled grace to fulfill and live. Doug Stringer writes in his book, *Somebody Cares: A Guide to Living Out Your Faith,* "While men reach for a throne to build their kingdoms, Jesus reached for a towel to wash men's feet."

Gloria Gadbury:
Mom to International Students

Gloria Gadbury and her husband are spiritual parents to dozens of international students who attend Christ for the Nations Institute in Dallas. Gloria and her husband attended CFNI thirty years ago and have been in ministry since then. They have an unusual ministry, as they aren't officially on staff with CFNI and don't receive any pay for what they do. Regardless, they are meeting basic needs and equipping students who will be ministers of the gospel in nations around the world. Gloria shares:

I am called "mom" by hundreds of students. For the international students, most of them have arrived in this country with very little financial support. They are on scholarships but have spent everything that they or their families could raise to send them to be trained in America.

What I am doing is laying my life down every day, picking up the cross and following Jesus. And what we are teaching the students, regardless of nation, is that they must do the same. Sometimes I don't want to do anything. But then there is a knock at the door and I have to answer it...with someone having need for food, a ride, and a prayer.

But God gives you the strength to come and do it. Tonight we are having twenty-eight over for a simple dinner of spaghetti. This will be the best meal that some of them will have had all week.

For the students we are spiritually parenting, all of them will learn to lay their life down when they return to the mission field, and for some of them it may mean that literally.

The servant leadership model is easy for spiritual moms to understand. Shepherding children, people, and projects is a natural expression of the gifts that moms have. Leadership in the Kingdom is not about power, position, or control; it is about serving others. Jesus said that the servant is the greatest of all.

Reaching Out

Spiritual moms know that releasing a person into his destiny can change a city, a nation, the world, and eternity. One day when I called Louise, one of my spiritual moms, she told me about a new prayer God had taught her. She shared with bubbling enthusiasm, "Lynn, you know God told me that He wanted me to pray some big prayers. He told me to pray big prayers, really big prayers. And I am!"

This is such great advice. Spiritual moms help teach others to have bigger vision, have bigger dreams, and pray bigger prayers.

You Can Be a
Spiritual Mom

Chapter Nine

Guidelines for Successful Spiritual Moms

The world needs more spiritually mature women! Where are they? There are more people in need of counseling than we can handle! This is the cry coming from pastors and other people in ministry. There is a huge need for mature men and women to act as mentors and simply be friends to someone in need. The high divorce rate, economic challenges, and parentless generations are only a few of the contributing factors to the growing numbers of those needing love and spiritual parenting. Even though the attendance at prayer circles, Bible studies, home fellowships, and cell groups are growing, the need for one-on-one mentoring continues to grow.

Why Don't Women Mentor More?

With such a growing need, why aren't there more spiritual moms and dads? There are many reasons. The biggest hindrances are time, lack of experience, and not knowing how to get started.

Gail Evans, former executive vice president at CNN and author of *She Wins, He Wins*, says the main reasons that women don't mentor in the work world are because they feel they don't have time, haven't been mentored themselves, or are waiting for the company or business system to "fix it" with a program, which usually doesn't work. Evans states, "Mentoring comes from the heart, not a program. Women are natural mentors but somehow forget about doing it when they are in the man's world. Mentoring other women needs to be part of every business woman's career strategy." Gail is correct about the importance of mentoring in business, but I believe that women need to make mentoring a lifestyle in every area of life.

Even though mentoring and spiritual mothering are natural extensions of the female personality, another big hesitation women have is because of "time wasters." Women wear so many hats that there doesn't seem to be any time for themselves. There is a legitimate concern that they don't want to be involved with someone who will take too much time and attention. This is an important point and valid concern. Many spiritual moms have had to deal with individuals who love to call several times a day and may not pick up on subtle and not-so-subtle hints that it may not be the best time to visit.

Marge and Ann—32 Years and Still Growing!

On the other hand, many spiritual moms and spiritual daughters are great examples of how to maintain balance in a relationship. Marge Thomas is 76 and Ann Hunter is 54. They have been spiritual mom and daughter for more than 32 years. They first met in California when Ann and her husband attended the church that Marge and her husband pastored. Their relationship got started one evening when Marge took dinner over to Ann's house when she was ill. With one casserole, they began a relationship that has continued even though they have both moved many times and have not lived in the same city for over 28 years.

Over the years their relationship has grown into a close friendship. They have great mutual admiration for each other. Like other spiritual moms, Marge will tell you that she is proud of Ann and that her spiritual daughter is doing more for the Lord than she ever dreamed possible.

In the beginning of their relationship, Marge was very busy with her kids, husband, and church and didn't have lots of time to spend on the phone. This didn't bother Ann because, "Marge never disappointed me even if she couldn't talk when I called. She taught me that my hope was in Jesus. She taught me even if she couldn't be there then God was always there."

Ann continues, "This meant that I wasn't looking to her to fix me but learned that God was my source, not another person. This focus also meant that she protected herself so that she didn't get drained. There are a lot of women who don't want to become spiritual mothers because they are afraid of people who are going to take up all their time and energy, and become like spiritual parasites."

Marge noticed that when she gave Ann Scripture or correction, Ann immediately took the Word and integrated it into her life. This made Marge realize that she was serious about serving the Lord, and eventually the spiritual mothering grew into a deep personal friendship with Ann and her family. In fact, Ann is totally accepted as one of the family by Marge's husband and children.

No Soup Principle

One of the most important lessons that Ann learned from Marge came when she taught her the basic spiritual mom principle of "Don't Rescue." Marge calls this the "No Soup" principle.

"Ann had the hardest time learning this and not understanding why you couldn't meet every need you saw. Until one day I explained to her it was like the story of the Prodigal Son. If Ann had lived next door and seen the Prodigal Son in the pigsty, she would have probably gone and taken him soup, which would have kept him from returning to the Father. From that point on, when we discussed Ann's rescuing certain people, if it was not a good situation, all we had to say was NO SOUP and she immediately backed off."

Their relationship is now more of a friendship. It continues to grow, and they spend many holidays together. Ann says that she doesn't know where she would be in her life if it weren't for Marge. "Anyone can quote Scripture all day. The reason Marge became a spiritual mother was because I wanted to see someone who walked and lived it every day."

Sometimes there are situations when spiritual mothering or mentoring doesn't work out like we had expected. Sometimes there are personality conflicts, growth resistance, and any number of things that cause disagreements.

Denise—Spiritual Mothering Isn't Always Easy

It was a wonderful summer morning, sunny and bright, and the morning temperatures were mild for a Texas June. I was excited because after months of invitations, conversations, and prayers, Denise was finally coming to church with me. I was happy because she had been going through a difficult time and needed to spend time in the company of saints. Even though we are the same age, I had been functioning as a spiritual mother and counselor to Denise for over a year.

Denise had been unemployed for months and had been desperately trying to find a job so that she wouldn't lose her house. She had great experience as a corporate executive assistant, with excellent organizational skills and knowledge. Unfortunately, Denise had been on dozens of interviews, frequently losing the position in the final interview.

We had been working on trusting the Lord, controlling negative talk, maintaining peace, and releasing critical attitudes. Like all of us, Denise had some areas that she needed to grow in, but God had given me a glimpse of who Denise could be in Christ. It just takes time for God to work in people's lives. That is the same hope that every spiritual mom builds upon. As spiritual parents, our portion is the hope of prisoners set free, bonds broken, blind eyes opened, and tongues singing praises to God.

That morning, as Denise pulled up to drive me to church, she explained that she had been up all night worrying and was too upset to go to church. I reassured her that church was exactly the place she needed to be and encouraged her to come in for at least part of the service. With someone else, I might have urged them to stay home in prayer, but having heard the same story before, I believed that this situation required a different response. Several other times I had asked Denise to come to church but she always had other excuses. This time I asked her to reconsider and said that I believed that church was exactly where she would find the answers.

I challenged her with Scripture, implored and begged her to reconsider, yet Denise still refused to go. I went to church alone and the service was wonderful. The sermon was all about crying out to God, and the pastor prayed for people who needed breakthrough in finances, relationships, and opportunities. It was as if the sermon had been custom-made for Denise. But she missed it. When I got home I emailed her and encouraged her to listen to the sermon on the website, and hoped she would.

Being a spiritual mom, you often have to draw a line in the sand for people and for yourself. This is never easy and never fun. Many times people want comfort; they want you to fix their problem for them. It is important to recognize this and not get hooked into an unhealthy dependent relationship.

As Marge Thomas states, "Spiritual moms don't need to be the Holy Spirit for people." Ann Barge adds, "People have to find their own solutions to problems and work them out in the way that is best for them." Some people may talk and act as if they want you to fix things, but this is not your role. Often people like Denise have a lot of fear and want to control everything around them, even the way God answers their prayers. Sometimes folks just have to come to the end of themselves before they get better.

As the father in the parable of the Prodigal Son demonstrated, parents have to release their children so that they can learn for themselves. This is a great spiritual truth that we all have to discover—the end of ourselves, the end of our resources, strengths, talents, gifts, energies, connections, tricks, formulas, and other personal parachutes. We usually make this discovery when we are at the edge of the cliff and have to jump off by faith into the arms of God.

One of the great "end of the rope" lessons that people learn is that they have to change "my will" to "Thy will." God's principles and commandments do not bend and change because we want them to. The "end of ourselves" is the opportunity God is waiting for so He can show us that He alone is our source and hope. Spiritual moms and dads are the ones who are cheering people on to take the leap of faith and finish the race.

That Sunday I realized something about my relationship with Denise. I realized that we had different expectations for our relationship. People respond differently to stress and have their own growth rate. As Doug Stringer of

Somebody Cares says, "Different expectations will destroy relationships." Different expectations had placed a wedge between Denise and myself.

Even though that Sunday with Denise did not go the way I had expected, there were lessons and reminders that are valuable. Mistakes are the gift package that many of life's lessons come in. We just have to take the time to let the Holy Spirit unwrap the gift in the "mistake package" and teach us how to use what is inside. The Bible promises, *"He who has begun a good work in you will complete it until the day of Jesus Christ"* (Philippians 1:6 NKJV).

So I took a step back and began evaluating the situation. I had to take a hard look as to why and how "in the name of kindness" I had misread the relationship. I started a list of life lessons and spoke to several wiser spiritual moms. Here are several lessons to help when you are operating in the role of a spiritual mom.

Lessons for Spiritual Moms

Point them in the right direction. It is important to always point people in the right direction—God's direction. They need to know that God is their source, Jesus is their hope, and the Holy Spirit will speak. Spiritual moms teach people to remember that the Word of God is their foundation, God's truth will light their path, and that their job is to bathe everything in prayer and worship.

Ann Hunter reminds us of what Marge did: "Marge was a pastor's wife with children, husband, and church to take care of and she didn't have much time. She taught me that even though she couldn't spend lots of time with me that God would always be there for me. If I called and she was busy I knew that God had a really great experience for me privately."

Beth Moore's spiritual mother, Marge Caldwell, who has been a Christian counselor for more than twenty years, explains, "It is important that a spiritual mom not try to be the Holy Spirit for people. People have to learn to find God's truth for themselves."

Find out what their spiritual level is. Just as a child or employee is evaluated, a person's spiritual walk must be measured to best meet their needs. Are they on a spiritual milk or meat diet? New believers have to be spoon-fed the Word and need you to spend time encouraging them. As people mature in Christ, they often only need you to point them to the right passage in Scripture and they are able to work out a solution.

Spiritual moms need to figure out if they are seeding, feeding, or weeding in a person's life. But whatever season, we always remember that everyone grows differently. When evaluating the spiritual maturity of a person, remember that Paul warned us to not treat the wealthy differently than the poor. Don't look at the externals, worldly success, strength, or achievements, because these things have nothing to do with spiritual maturity or understanding.

Find out if they have a sincere desire to grow. Watch them walk—the talk is not as important. Test them to see if they are willing to grow or if they are looking for you to make them feel better. Sometimes people just want you to change their diapers so they can go make another mess.

Clarify the expectations for the relationship. Sometimes all people need is a weekly or monthly phone call to keep on track; other times people need more hands-on involvement. A spiritual mom knows that her availability must be in sync with the person's needs. This is not something you can plan, because when God brings someone into your life, He will make the time. As Ann Barge explains, "Often I don't know what I am to do or say to a person until they show up. Then God will take over and I will know exactly what book or Scripture they need or what to pray."

When in a spiritual parenting situation, be sure that you have covered the basics with people. Don't take anything for granted or assume they know the basics of salvation, Scripture, or godly principles. Make sure they are saved. Do they know how to read the Word or pray? Are they in a small group? Are they committed to a church body or just church jumpers looking for instant answers and spiritual fast food? Do they have deeper personal issues that need the help of a pastor or professional counselor? Prayerfully refer them elsewhere if you are not equipped to help.

Love your neighbor as yourself. It is important that we love our neighbors as ourselves. Even though we need to be patient and longsuffering, it is important that we don't let our families and ourselves be used and abused. Discernment and boundaries are critical to our success in parenting, mentoring, and life.

One of my friends has been in ministry with her husband for years. Some of their grown children have some deep anger against their parents because they feel their parents were away from home too much during their childhood. Even though some of these feelings may not be based on truth, children can be wounded when they perceive that their needs are not being met. It's important to keep a balance and dialogue open with our families to make sure that they are comfortable with our level of involvement with others. There is always a high premium on a mother's time and attention. A mom's love is one of the greatest prescriptions in the world; that's why there is always a demand.

Boundaries are critical. We must be careful how much we say yes and how much we say no in order to make sure that we are not continually drained. Our time is valuable, and we need to make sure that we are spending it wisely. Of course, there are situations that require years of dedication before fruit is seen, and the Lord will give us grace in situations like these. A spiritual mothering situation needs to show fruit and progress, but it doesn't always happen immediately. Remember who is the Lord of the harvest. Marge Caldwell shares, "The worst thing you can do is become an enabler with someone. You can't help a person if they remain the way they are. My counseling experiences have shown that when people are depressed they can become very selfish about things. There is a real danger point."

People who have been traumatized or are deeply in need are often not able to appropriately establish boundaries. We must recognize and set those boundaries for families and ourselves—not allowing other people to make claims on time that is committed to other priorities. Spiritual moms remind us that phone calls and continual crises in the lives of others must not be allowed to consume our family time. (For more information, see the book *Boundaries* by Henry Cloud and John Townsend.)

As my grandfather taught me, it is important to "Love 'em the way they are." But when we are in a relationship, this does not mean that we should tolerate selfish behaviors, poor manners, disrespect, or ungratefulness when we have given of our families' time and ourselves.

Ask God to give you a love in your heart for the people He wants you to mentor and the strength to say no to those people who aren't supposed to be taking your time.

Marge Caldwell gives the perfect perspective with this important point: "Remember that people didn't get into their messes overnight. It is going to take more than one session or evening to fix it. Sometimes you have to remind them that it will take time to heal and solve this problem."

Spiritual moms are great at knowing how to do several things at the same time. Ann Hunter shares what she learned. "One day I had some important questions and I went to Syble Griffing, my pastor's wife. She was working through a long list but invited me to jump in the car and talk while she ran an errand. We talked as we walked through the mall and store. By the time we got back from this 45-minute trip, I had all my questions answered and was given a great example of how spiritual moms handle things. Syble was still doing life!"

Just because a person needs to talk doesn't mean that you have to drop everything you are doing. Years ago in graduate school, I needed to talk with Ann Barge but she was in the middle of her Saturday list. She had to clean the refrigerator. When I came over I began to help her with her chore. I was thrilled to clean the refrigerator as she counseled me. Now when I visit her house every year or two, cleaning the refrigerator has become an activity that I do to bless her.

If I have a young person who wants to have a long talk, I don't have to stop what I am doing to listen. Often they will join me as I cook, clean the garage, sort through files, or work in the yard. If they show a commitment to help me deal with the dirt in my garage, I will be happy to help them with their internal dirt. This is a great measure of friendship and gives me a greater understanding of their character and work habits. They get my time and counsel and I get some help with my chores. Spiritual moms know that you can do life at the same time!

Encourage them to pray the Lord's Prayer and really mean it. The Lord's Prayer is still the best prayer for helping people. Counseling, Bible study, prayer, fellowship, worship, and service are all tools that can help heal the spirit. But the first and most important step to freedom from the emotional chains of the past is the simple line,

Forgive us our trespasses as we forgive those who trespass against us.

As a spiritual mom, I have to first walk in forgiveness, humility, and the love of Christ in order to teach this to others. Learning to forgive others and ourselves is the door that leads to freedom. It is only through the love and power of God that we can truly forgive and walk in the peace that passes understanding. Spiritual moms know that taking a person's hand and leading them on the path of prayer is the most important road of all.

Help them to grow in responsibility. Don't rescue! Spiritual moms have to be tough, especially with willful adults. They know that raising kids is a tough job and the same is true with spiritual children, especially when they are over 40. Make sure that you are spirit-led in helping people and not driven by manipulation or crisis. Remember that only God can change them, not you.

People will be appreciative of your help, but don't let it go to your head. Be cautious when you hear individuals say, "I don't know what I would have done without you." Profuse praise, flattery, and gratitude can be attractive coverings for the "rescue-me" hook and "fix-it-for-me" trap. My job as a spiritual mom is to point them to the real source that is Christ.

Marge Thomson gives this final reminder: "There are lots of people who are rescuers. But if you are a child of God, you are led by the Spirit of God and do what He calls you to do. It is important to give when God tells you to give, but don't always go out there and rescue them. If we go out and pull someone out of a lesson before it is finished, then God has to start all over again."

Just as natural parents establish boundaries, spiritual parents have guidelines that lead to success. Understanding those guidelines will help prevent disappointment and encourage growth. The goal is to raise mature Christians with an active faith. Spiritual moms know that their advice must always be God-centered, spirit-led, and scripturally based. Spiritual moms remember that it is God who changes a person and that rescuing doesn't work. Their objective is to help people grow into mature Christians who will help multiply the Kingdom and love God with all their heart, soul, mind, and strength.

Gayle Miller

Gayle Miller is one of those women that many of us want to be when we grow up. She is beautiful, gracious, and intelligent, and when she speaks everyone around her stops to listen to her soft, clear voice. It is amazing that someone this kind and generous was able to succeed in the cutthroat world of fashion. But after spending a few minutes listening to Gayle's observations and tough questions, you feel it's a wonder they ever let her retire.

Gayle is the former president of Anne Klein II, which changed the image of career woman. Through her leadership AKII developed a philosophy and strategy that revolutionized wardrobes for the growing population of career women. By using classic designs and carrying forward colors and themes, a woman was able to progressively build a wardrobe that projected a feminine and professional image.

One of the reasons why AKII was so successful was that, on the advice of her management-consultant husband and because of what she learned through experience, Gayle developed a management style that was very progressive for that time. She built a team of people who each brought their own expertise and creativity. All of the thirteen team members shared in responsibility for establishing goals and leading. Competition was focused towards the market rather than internally. This "community" approach strengthened the team's loyalty and performance.

Now that she has retired, Gayle has turned a great deal of her energies toward helping young people in the Los Angeles public schools. The fashion world's loss is the gain of today's kids. Gayle is helping to build the future by investing in hundreds of thousands of students. Gayle has helped with developing and implementing multiple projects in the areas of foundational development, reading programs, mother/girl mentoring, working with at-risk youth, charter schools, and Christian mentoring.

The Blueprint for Living is a value-based curriculum that has reached over 500,000 kids in the Los Angeles area. The mother/daughter program has helped mentor mothers and daughters at the Junior High School level, which is a critical time of intervention for young girls. Gayle is very busy helping build relationships and teams that will help carry these programs forward into the future. She says, "It is very exciting on lots of levels. We have formed a strategic network, which is starting its own network of charter schools. In the next five years we anticipate launching fifty schools in the area."

In addition, Gayle helps mentor several groups of women. The weekly groups meet for both Bible study and prayer. Being in the LA area, Gayle often meets women in the entertainment business. In fact, the Media Fellowship group in which Gayle is involved helps to mentor young actresses and actors. They have seen lots of answers to prayer and many restored marriages. Whether praying with a young actress or coordinating a foundation, Gayle is a spiritual mother who is being used by God to change her community.

Chapter Ten

Sing, O Barren Woman

"Sing, O barren woman,
you who never bore a child;
burst into song, shout for joy,
you who were never in labor;
because more are the children of the desolate woman
than of her who has a husband,"
says the LORD.
—Isaiah 54:1 NIV

Creating a training school for young people in the foster care system is the last thing Ida Moses thought she would be doing to serve the Lord. When Ida Moses thought of how she would serve the Lord, she assumed that because of her accounting background she would be used in an administrative manner. But God had other plans. Ida has created a training school for young people in the foster care system to teach them bookkeeping and other office skills

In November of 1981, Ida woke up from a dream saying, "Right hand, left hand, right hand, left hand." She didn't know what it meant. Then the Lord told her to open Isaiah 54 and read it. She had never read it before.

Ida read the Scripture: *"More are the children of the desolate woman than of her who has a husband."* She read that and thought, "That is a crazy Scripture and could never happen to me. I don't think that verse is right. How can I have lots of children—after all, I'm older and single?" So she turned over and went back to sleep.

Ten years later, before Christmas, Ida was teaching a Bible study for professionals in Washington, D.C. A phone call came, asking if someone could come and teach a Bible study in a nearby foster home. Ida said yes and asked if she and the group could bring gifts and food also.

So this group of professionals showed up one Tuesday to have a Bible study. There were about 30 rough-looking kids, looking as if they didn't want to be there. The adults had brought food, which made the young crowd more receptive. Ida shares, "We found out later that at that first meeting they paid the kids to be there. But soon this little weekly study became standing room only."

At the first Bible study, they studied the life of Joseph. The kids embraced the story because they could understand the pain that Joseph went through. Ida says that young people in the foster care system know several things—your family can fail you, life is unpredictable, and the system can fail you. She says, "At the end of the first study we all joined hands to pray for any requests. I was a bit stunned when one of young men asked, 'Please pray that when I turn 21, I won't be homeless.' Many of the other kids nodded in agreement." Ida shares:

What I discovered was that the foster care system in Washington, D.C., is set up so that when a person turns 21 they are cut off from funding and released from the system, whether or not they have a place to go or a place to stay. Many of these kids don't have support, so many become homeless and turn to crime or prostitution to survive. Our group didn't know what to do except to keep having the weekly Bible study and love the kids. We taught the Word and began to see many of the young people give their lives to the Lord. But through it all, these kids would come in with their friends and want prayer—prayer for their life beyond the foster system, because they didn't know how they were going to survive.

The turning point for me happened because of Myra. Myra was an attractive young girl with a flair for dressing, but she tended to dress too seductively. When she first attended, she said she was an atheist. Still, she came faithfully every week and sat by the door. After several months she made a commitment for Christ.

With time, as with many of the kids, we heard her story. Myra had entered the foster care system at the age of three. She had hoped that she would be adopted, but it never happened. It was a very hard life.

Then one evening Myra came dressed totally differently. Instead of a cute outfit, she was wearing large coveralls with long legs and sleeves. When I asked her about it she showed me that she had her normal clothes on under the jumpsuit. The reason she was wearing it was, as she explained, "This was my last day in foster care and tonight I turn homeless. I will be 21 in four months so I will be homeless then, anyway, besides I'm not getting along with my counselor."

I said, "Myra, hang in there for four more months and it will be better." Myra said, "I'm not afraid; I'm going to make it." That night we prayed for her after the study and invited her back. She left and I have never seen her again.

Over the weeks that we kept looking for Myra, it began to haunt me. What if I had a program that would have kept her from living on the streets? So I decided to start one. I took a segment of my CPA office and set up a place to train young people to be bookkeepers. That was the beginning of Based In Love Ministries. Our focus is to give vocational skills to young people in the foster care system so that they have a way to make a living and build a life for themselves. We show them the love of Christ. We teach them that they do have what it takes to be somebody. Bookkeeping is the hook. But what really happens is that we become the family that these young men and women never had.

They come in one way but they leave as whole, entirely different young people. Year after year, they continue to come back to visit and hang around. One day, several years after we had gotten the program started, I looked up in my office and noticed that there were kids all over the place. My business office was like Grand Central Station and I was walking around the office singing.

I have never been one to stand up and sing, but now there is such a song in my heart. It was then that I remembered the middle of the night when I read Isaiah 54 more than twenty years ago. God told me that night that I would have a lot of children; but I believe that it is only the beginning of the manifestation of the promise.

I believe that "*Sing, O barren woman, because more are the children of the desolate woman than of her who has a husband. Enlarge your territory,*" was written about me.

*****

There are some pieces of Scripture that stick in your memory every time you read them. You know what I mean: you are sitting down to read your Bible and it opens up to a passage, which you've read six times in the past two months. As you read the passage again, POW! a new truth hits you right between the eyes and it is time for a "Selah moment." Time to pause, reflect, and camp out at this address in the Bible. So pull up a chair, cup of coffee, clipboard, and concordance, because God has something you need to hear.

Isaiah 54 is one of those places for me.

"Sing, O barren woman,
    you who never bore a child;
burst into song, shout for joy,
    you who were never in labor;
because more are the children of the desolate woman

than of her who has a husband,"
says the LORD.

"Enlarge the place of your tent,
*   stretch your tent curtains wide,*
*   do not hold back;*
lengthen your cords,
*   strengthen your stakes.*
For you will spread out to the right and to the left;
*   your descendants will dispossess nations*
*   and settle in their desolate cities.*

"Do not be afraid; you will not suffer shame.
*   Do no fear disgrace; you will not be humiliated.*
You will forget the shame of your youth
*   and remember no more the reproach of your widow-*
hood.
For your Maker is your husband,
*   the LORD Almighty is his name—*
the Holy One of Israel is your Redeemer;
*   he is called the God of all the earth."*
—Isaiah 54:1–5 NIV

Isaiah 54 is one of my life chapters. I have wept, laughed, prayed, sung, danced, shouted, declared, and rejoiced with these promises again and again. Many spiritual moms and women agree that this chapter speaks to their hearts and gives them hope and encouragement.

These verses touch me because I never had a biological child, and would be considered physically "barren." Since I was a little girl, I wanted first and foremost to be a mom. Early on I decided to have five kids and started praying at seventeen for twins. I chose five kids because growing up there were two families on our block that had five kids, and it was the biggest number of kids that I could imagine a woman birthing and still retaining her looks. (Though I have several friends with six and eight kids and they look great.) In short, I love children any size, shape, or condition. My books and spending money in college came from babysitting, counseling, and teaching. I attended seminary with the primary focus of using my master's degree in theatre to enrich Sunday school programs and outreach efforts to children.

After college I worked at a theatre school and transitioned into the television industry. After getting a career up and rolling, I married an older man with teens, so we put my biological time clock on snooze for a couple of years. When it came time to start our family, my spouse changed his mind about having children. The combination of this decision with other challenges led us down the painful path of divorce.

Sterile Choices

My career as a news consultant took off, and I was on the road more than 170 days a year. Business was great, but I never found the right person to marry. In my late thirties, I considered adoption and even produced a video on international adoption, which has helped unite hundreds of overseas orphans and parents. But every one of my adoption attempts ended in frustration. No matter how hard I tried, I wasn't able to have children. Career choices and personal mistakes took me on paths away from that which I desired.

Every year between Christmas and New Year's, I spend at least one long evening alone with God. This is the time to reflect on the year, read my journals and sermon notes, pray, and try to listen to the Lord. Many years I have spent a portion of the evening time crying and asking God why I wasn't able to have a husband or child. It didn't make sense that a person like me who adored children and desired above all to be a great mother would not be able to have them.

I understand in part the pain that Sarah, Hannah, Rachel, and Elizabeth must have felt. Barrenness is a dull ache that starts at your heart but eventually pulls at every fiber of your self, until you are a portrait of sorrows, hanging onto the threads of God's promises. You have to hold onto God and push beyond the envy of invitations for baby showers and the pain of childless Mother's Days. You have to take those baby blankets and darling outfits out of the bottom drawer and give them away before you start crying. You have to trust and fear God enough to say no to trying to conceive a child of your will, even though there may never be a child of God's will.

Even though having children was one of the greatest desires of my heart, there was a Christmas several years ago where I had to put my hope for a child on the altar. If God would require even Abraham to offer up the son of his dreams, then can He expect anything less from me? Every goal, dream, and expectation in our life has to be laid upon the altar so that God can give it back to us. I had to give my "right" to have a child up to the Lord so that His work could be done in me. Even though this was a bitter pill to swallow, in doing so I received peace and freedom from bitterness against God and others.

It Wasn't Time Yet!

That Christmas night when I surrendered my hope for a child, I read Isaiah 54 and loudly reminded God of His Word and asked Him to give me thousands of spiritual children for all the physical ones that were missing from my life. It was then I heard a whisper: "I have not allowed you to be a mother of few so that you could be a mother of multitudes." I stopped, took a deep breath, and started singing and weeping at the same time, not knowing if I had heard correctly.

That Sunday, I was visiting Shady Grove Church and went up to say hello to the founding pastor, Olen Griffing. We had met several years earlier at a conference, but I had never been to a Sunday service. He said to me, "I know that you know about Sarah, Elizabeth, and Hannah, and what their condition was like. But you know they really weren't barren. It just wasn't God's time yet for them to give birth. You need to remember that they weren't barren, it just wasn't time yet." I was shocked and returned to my seat. My heart swelled with the promise, "It wasn't time yet!"

Now, years later, I have entered a new season. I moved to Shady Grove and have been blessed with wonderful relationships, and the Lord is bringing many spiritual daughters into my life. My house is always buzzing with activities, Bible studies, prayer meetings, potlucks, and guests. For years I have prayed that my house would be a place of healing and rest, and that is exactly what happens when people visit. Isaiah 54 has taken on an entirely new meaning in my life, and I am still looking for the multitudes.

So as a barren woman whom God has made to sing, I'm offering to you my version of Isaiah 54. This is from the spiritual mom amplified semi-jazzing version.

****

Hey gals, be happy and turn up the praise music, all you sisters. Sing as loud as you can. God is about to have a party, and you are the hostess du jour! Ask God to enlarge your heart because the gang is coming. Increase your flexibility, roll out the sofa bed, and keep a casserole and extra pizza in the freezer. Make sure you have your grocery coupons ready, and don't worry about leftovers 'cause there won't be any. Be sure to add extra plates to the table and invite those "lonely faces, singles, and single moms" over after church or for a cup of coffee. Don't worry about formal china right now, but use the disposable plates because people time is better than kitchen time.

Spiritual children love to talk all hours of the day and night. So remember, sleep is highly overrated and has nothing to do with beauty. Stay up late to counsel, and have popcorn and snacks ready.

Remember to simplify and unclutter your house, inside and out, so you can make room for others. Don't let your possessions keep you in a prison. Don't be concerned about the house cleaning that didn't get done when you have been scrubbing up a soul for the Lord. Kids take time, and when a family is under construction no one cares that things are a little messy. After all, it is only temporary.

Strengthen your foundation so you are prepared for them when they come. Lengthen your prayer lists and put out those extra books to help others. Strengthen your knowledge of the Word. Drive the Word into your life so that it is a sure foundation for whatever storm may be blowing through the lives of those you counsel. It will make no difference because you're anchored in the rock-solid gospel knowledge of Christ.

Fresh bread and fresh prayer are important. "I need you, Lord," should be your daily prayer to God. You may not have a clue about what is going on, but don't worry. Enjoy the ride and learn to laugh more. The joy of the Lord will be your strength. Laughing with folks may be the quickest way to heal them. So get out the board games, cards, and funny movies, and have fun.

****

Blessing of Barrenness

It was in late summer before 9/11, and Joann Cole Webster and our publicity team had been working day and night getting ready for the historic Global Celebration for Women. One late morning, Joann called me and told me that she had just gotten a new revelation about the "barren womb" in Proverbs 30. The Scripture reads,

> *There are three things that are never satisfied,*
> *four that never say, "Enough!":*
> *the grave, the barren womb,*
> *land, which is never satisfied with water,*
> *and fire, which never says, "Enough!"*
> —Proverbs 30:15b–16 NIV

Joann and I have never had biological children, yet we have often discussed and prayed together about having children. Joann has had a very busy life personally and in ministry. For the early years of her marriage, she helped raise two stepsons. At the same time, she worked alongside her father, Dr. Edwin Louis Cole, authoring 18 books and helping expand the Christian Men's Network into 221 nations. For five years she was the CEO of this ministry that was dedicated to discipling men around the globe.

Joann is a great stepmother to her grown stepsons and actively mentors all of her nieces, nephews, and dozens of other young women and men. Joann shared that she had just gotten a new insight about the hunger that a barren womb must be like. We discussed how this passage gave the impression that as childless women we would never be satisfied and fulfilled. As barren women, our children had become the people we mentored and the projects or books we created.

Joann said that during her quiet time she had turned her focus from the biological or natural womb into a spiritual womb. In the physical, a "barren" womb can never be satisfied because it is always longing for children. In the spiritual context, then, the "barren" womb can never be satisfied but always wants more spiritual children and will never have enough.

What this means is that physical barrenness becomes a blessing because it creates a hunger for spiritual children that can never be satisfied. A physically barren woman can never have enough spiritual children and kingdom fruit to satisfy her longing and desire.

Joann and I realized that working with projects like the Global Celebration, which united women from 167-plus nations across denominational, racial, and socio-economic backgrounds, was an extension of our spiritual wombs. We were helping to birth something that would save souls, transform communities, and change the world.

Now, several years later, I understand this even more deeply. My heart longs to see people living in the freedom and peace that comes only from a deep, abiding relationship with Christ. My heart aches sometimes when I pray over people. My mouth can't stop telling people all the wonderful things that God has done.

God Himself has put a fire inside of me that will not be quenched. God has put a thirst for His presence that will not be satisfied. God has put a hunger for His Word that will not be filled. God has challenged me to take my selfishness to the grave every day. God has replaced my barren womb with a spiritual one that is full of life and always hungry. The barrenness has been turned into blessings, which will never shout out, "Enough!"

Spiritual Mothering out of Barrenness

In talking with spiritual moms, I found that many of them had deep compassion that was often a result of previous pain that they experienced. Spiritual moms, time after time, would tell me that they wanted to help other people through a difficult time because of what they had been through.

Years ago, I had surgery and had to go through it all by myself. There was no one to even help hold the bedpan when I was sick. So now whenever someone is going to the hospital, I make sure that they have someone with them. I want to make sure that other people don't have the same fears and loneliness.
—Women's Pastor Kaye Green, Shady Grove Church

I make sure that whenever any of my spiritual daughters have a baby, I am at the hospital. I also take time off work to stay with them for two weeks after the baby is born. When I had my son, I was very sad and alone because I didn't have a mother to be with me. She had died many years before, and I know how depressing it can be to be alone with a baby and no family.
—Macy Domingo, TV and radio host, Cote D'Ivoire

I want to make sure my nephews and niece are taught ways to communicate and that their faith is rooted in Jesus, even though they are still in preschool. When I was young, I wasn't taught to communicate clearly, and I want to make sure that they are better equipped.
—Misty Woodruff, publicist

My kids and I are going to buy cars, fix them up, and give them to single moms who need them. Not being able to have a reliable vehicle was always a big stress for me as a single mom with four kids.
—Debbie Bohn, single mom of four.

Barren Womb Births Compassion
It is said that we understand best that which we experience and walk through. Spiritual moms have compassion, which translates into loving actions. Just as we experience

the birth pangs before a child is born, Spiritual moms have often experienced the same pain that others are going through and have compassion for them, which translates into a desire to serve and love others.

It is interesting to look at the Hebrew roots for the term "barren womb" from Proverbs 30:16. The word for womb is *rachem,* which means "womb" or "compassion." In the verb form, it means to love deeply, have mercy, be compassionate, and have tender affections (tender mercies of our Lord).

The word for *barren* means "restraint," "oppression," or "prison." This comes together to say that, when we turn the curse of "barrenness" over to God, it is replaced and births instead compassion, deep love, affection, and tender mercy in the spiritual dimension.

In God the barren womb can be the ignition switch to an outpouring of tremendous love, compassion, and actions. Often spiritual moms have no idea what the results of their mothering will be, because it grows from an unlimited source of divine love.

Spiritual moms are women who have turned the pain of life experiences and barrenness into actions fueled by compassion and filled with love. Spiritual moms are always expanding the territory around their homes and hearts. Even for women who may not have children or whose children are not at home, God wants to transform their lives into spiritual wombs that will never cry "enough" when gathering souls for the Kingdom.

Chapter Eleven

Women, Words, and Worship

Though I speak with the tongues of men and of angels, but have not love, I have become sounding brass or a clanging cymbal.
—1 Corinthians 13:1 NKJV

One day a successful young man came to a rabbi to ask him for counsel. The young man was known for his quick temper and biting words. The rabbi asked the young man to bring a pillow with him as they walked to a tower. "Strange request," thought the young man, "but of course, the rabbi is old and needs a little cushion for his frame. The bench by the belfry is very hard."

The young man smiled to himself and wondered if people noticed how thoughtful he was, graciously carrying a pillow for the rabbi as they walked through the town. They climbed to the top of the tower and watched how the swallows danced over the fields and the wind waltzed in the willows. After a few minutes of hearing a list of the young man's complaints about others, the rabbi picked up the pillow from the bench where the young man had placed it. The rabbi walked to the edge of the tower and ripped the pillow. Gusts of wind grabbed the feathers so that they rose up like a cloud, then scattered across the fields.

The rabbi turned slowly to the young man and said, "My son, can you bring back the feathers for me?" The young man swallowed hard, irritated that the rabbi had ruined a perfectly good pillow. "No, rabbi, you know that is impossible." "My son, your words are like the feathers. Once you release them you cannot get them back. So be careful what you release into the winds of life, for you never know how far a feather or word may go."

The Power of Words

Our words have great power. In building Christian character, one of the greatest areas of discipline is in the area of the tongue. All of us have released words into the wind that we wish we could bring back. Spiritual moms help people learn how to speak life, not death. Along with developing a renewed mind and an attitude of forgiveness, controlling the tongue makes the list of "top ten things that need overhaul."

Even the Bible agrees that controlling the tongue is tough:

> *But no man can tame the tongue. It is an unruly evil, full of deadly poison. With it we bless our God and Father, and with it we curse men, who have been made in the similitude of God. Out of the same mouth proceed blessing and cursing. My brethren, these things ought not to be so.*
> —James 3:8–10 NKJV

But when the words are redeeming, the tongue is life-giving.

> *The words of a man's mouth are deep waters;*
> *The wellspring of wisdom is a flowing brook.*
> —Proverbs 18:4 NKJV

Controlling Words

Learning to control this area produces life. Good words produce life in our relationships, attitudes, spiritual growth, marriages, and businesses—everywhere. Scripture says that you reap what you sow and in the harvest of words, this is often painfully true. Spiritual moms are great at pointing out both the fruit and root of a naughty tongue. Andrea Taylor shares this story.

> I needed help with controlling my words, especially when it came to my husband. From the beginning of our marriage I had called him a degrading word. It got so bad that he even started referring to himself with that word. My spiritual mom pointed out how wrong this was. Finally the Lord convicted me and I had to go to God and my husband and ask him to forgive me for how I had dishonored him. What was interesting was that for thirteen years we had been trying to have a daughter. Not long after I had repented to my husband, I became pregnant with our daughter.

Andrea was fortunate that her spiritual mom had the courage to tell her the truth. Andrea showed humility and a teachable spirit. It takes time to change our words and the attitudes that created them. Having a spiritual mom who loves us enough to point out our blind spots and who cares enough to keep us accountable is a blessing.

Women: God-Made Communicators

Ladies, let's get right to it...most of us love to talk. Just ask our husbands or bosses. We love to visit with friends, family, mothers, daughters, sisters, other relatives, neighbors, business associates, and the delivery person. Some of us only like to talk to those people we like, while many of us will talk to anyone, anytime, anywhere, about anything.

If you haven't noticed, men and women are usually very different when it comes to conversations. Men usually prefer the headline version—pertinent facts without the whole story. Women want the "Gone with the Wind" version with a ticker tape commentary of "How did they feel?" running at the bottom of the screen. Different personalities also communicate differently. Regardless of personality type, words often reveal what is in a person's heart, both good and bad.

If anyone among you thinks he is religious, and does not bridle his tongue but deceives his own heart, this one's religion is useless.
—James 1:26 NKJV

But those things which proceed out of the mouth come from the heart, and they defile a man. For out of the heart proceed evil thoughts, murders, adulteries, fornications, thefts, false witness, and blasphemies.
—Matthew 15:18–19 NKJV

The Weight of Words

Women tend to talk and communicate more than men do. Research tells us that men will speak about 10,000–12,000 words a day, while a woman will say 20,000–24,000 words in a day. Women have bigger vocabularies in certain areas, like colors and decorations. Men will call something blue that women would call teal, royal, sea foam, French, denim, or turquoise. When women ask men to talk about feelings, men say, "I'm hungry, cold, tired, or good."

From the delivery room, the sexes show their difference. Little boys have to be wrapped carefully because they are often kicking and moving. Little girls are often born moving their lips. Men are more physical and women are more verbal. Men like to take action and women want to talk about it first.

God made men with the strength and ability to fight for territory. God made women to nurture and build community. Women have more words because it takes more words to teach children, manage a family, encourage a husband, and coordinate social activities.

"Women don't realize the power that they have been given through their words," explains publisher/author Joann Cole Webster. "Women think because they are the 'physically weaker sex' that it means that they are weak spiritually. They don't realize that when they speak God's Word they become mighty in the spirit realm. The enemy is afraid of women who are willing to pray God's will on earth as it is in heaven. Pray the Scriptures over their husbands, families, children, jobs, and communities."

Why Did God Give Women So Many Words?

The bottom line reason that women were given more words was to build the Kingdom. God wants women to use those words to plant seed, feed the body, build, equip, heal, love, worship, praise, and pray.

Spiritual moms know that life and death are in the tongue. Learning to control it is a lifelong growth process for everyone, but when we have victory, it is worth it. The first step in learning to control our speech is recognizing the spiritual value of words. In a world filled with too many words, it is easy to forget the power that words can have. Words are more than just sounds; when used for God's purposes, they can touch heaven, move mountains, heal the sick, and set prisoners free. God gave women an extra measure of words so that women would use them for His purposes. God wants women to redeem their communication gifts for Kingdom construction.

Why Are Words Important?

Words are the building blocks of communication. Communication is like the electricity in your house. Without it you can't see when it is dark, fix things, work on your computer, watch TV, or run the vacuum to clean the house. Like electricity, we depend upon words to help us do everything in our lives. Even when we are silent our brains are using words to make decisions. But before we think of what words are to people, consider how important words are to God.

> *In the beginning was the Word, and the Word was with God, and the Word was God. He was with God in the beginning. Through him all things were made; without him nothing was made that has been made.*
> —John 1:1–3 NIV

Words are the beginning of everything—by the Word the worlds were created. The Word is the name that the Gospel of John uses for God's Son. When God speaks, things happen. Stars are hung in the heavens. Continents are formed. Life begins. Man and woman were made. Using words is part of the divine nature of God. The Father shared this attribute with His children. When God breathed life into man's nostrils he became a "living being." Some Hebrew translations define this as "speaking spirit." As God breathed His life into us, He gave the human race something that no other creature has—the gift of speech. Speech is God's gift that allows us to share in the divine joy of communication and communion with Him.

When a baby is born, it greets the world with a cry. An infant uses its lungs and voice to tell us what it needs, wants, and fears. As we grow, we shape our world and life through our words. Now that we are adults, what are we crying out for? Sometimes our attempts at communication yield a good harvest, a wonderful marriage, or loving friendships. Sometimes we discover that our fields have been blighted by bitterness, anger, and disappointment.

Words Are Gifts, Protection, and Weapons

God promised that His Word would not return to Him void (Isaiah 55:10–11). What an incredible privilege God has given to us. He allows us to participate in speaking His Word so that a person may receive it and become born again.

• Words are the tools God gives us to plant faith and equip others. Words are spiritual gifts, tools, weapons, and the way we reach God.

• Words are the gifts God gave us to communicate with Him through prayer, praise, and worship. Words form the ladder that helps us reach toward heaven in love and adoration.

• Words are protection for the mind, thoughts, and faith, forming a part of a Christian's spiritual armor. *"Take the helmet of salvation and the sword of the Spirit, which is the word of God."* (Ephesians 6:17 NIV)

• When we speak, the Word of God provides defense and helps us to discern truth. *"For the word of God is living and powerful, and sharper than any two-edged sword, piercing even to the division of soul and spirit, and of joints and marrow, and is a discerner of the thoughts and intents of the heart"* (Hebrews 4:12 NKJV).

• The Word of our testimony defeats the enemy because it illuminates the power of God's truth so that the hearer may believe. *"They overcame him by the blood of the Lamb and by the word of their testimony; they did not love their lives so much as to shrink from death"* (Revelation 12:11 NIV).

• Testimony only happens when it is spoken. This means that God will use our testimonies to give victory in our lives. Spiritual moms must encourage others to testify and share with others what He has done. Learning to do this is a key to building a person's faith.

Praying for Trucks

I look for every opportunity to teach my nephews and nieces about God. One day I was sitting outside with my nephews, who were about four and five at the time. I was teaching them how to pray for things that we heard. I told them to close their eyes and listen. They told me they heard trucks, so I said let's pray for the men in the trucks and that they would know Jesus. Then one of the boys immediately folded his hands and got on his knees to pray. It was so wonderful. I knew that I was seeing the fruit of what I had helped plant in his life. I was like a proud parent.

—Misty Woodruff, aunt, spiritual mom, and public relations director.

We have been blessed in America to have so many incredible women who have plowed the spiritual ground of our nation through prayer. Over the decades there have been prayer ministries and events birthed through women such as Evelyn Christiansen, Vonette Bright, Shirley Dobson, and Catherine Marshall. We need to thank God for the millions of hours of prayer that these spiritual mothers and countless others in our nation have poured out at the Lord's feet.

Spiritual mothers help to teach, recruit, and train more intercessors to help fortify the prayer walls. Today we have more books on prayer, prayer resources, organizations, and conferences for prayer training than ever before. Through the Internet, prayer teams are weaving incredible nets of blessing around our world. Within seconds, people learn of needs and begin to pray. But there is still much to be done. Evelyn Christiansen explains, "When we are convicted by the idea that those without Jesus are lost eternally— whether it's a child rebelling and rejecting God, a struggling family member who won't accept Him, or a person who's never heard of Him—this is when we bombard heaven unceasingly" (quoted from *100 Christian Women Who Changed the Twentieth Century* by Helen Hosier, page 26).

It's All About Worship

Worship music is not just some kind of Christian substitute for worldly music. In worship, music is released for its true purposes of God. In fact, the battle in this world is all about worship. Dr. Diane Wigstone, in her book *Hope for Hollywood*, explains, "Hollywood is all about making images. Who will you worship? God, or the next big Hollywood star? Who will you desire, and let your thoughts dwell on?" That is why Satan offered all the kingdoms of this world to Christ, if He would only, "Bow down and worship me." Heaven is filled with sounds of worship; it is what we shall be doing for eternity.

Music has an amazing power to communicate to a person's spirit and heart when words fail. God must love music because He made so much of it. The power of music and worship is like rain upon the dry ground. Without the rain the seeds will never grow. Worship helps to refresh the soil and soften the hardest of hearts. The Father loves to sing over us (Zephaniah 3:17). When God spoke the words of creation, I wonder if they were spoken, or were they sung?

Worship opens hearts, lifts hearts, touches the heart of the Father. Worship is one of the greatest mysteries, greatest joys, and greatest spiritual weapons. Teaching people to worship in spirit and truth is an important objective for spiritual moms.

There have been many women of worship throughout the Scriptures. On their escape from Egypt, Miriam led the people of Israel with song and timbrel, dancing in victory. Deborah the judge sang a great prophetic song of victory. Mary sang a song of thanksgiving in what we call the Magnificat.

Today churches everywhere are filled with wonderful worshipping women. Our next profile will be with a "spiritual mum" of worship, Darlene Zschech of Hillsong, Australia, who is "Shouting to the Lord" and seeing worship transform lives.

☙

Darlene Zschech: Spiritual Mum

In today's revival, there is a fresh new wave of music washing around the world. The "new song" of worship is a unifying force of the body of Christ. You can visit churches on many continents and hear the same music being sung at Baptist churches, Catholic churches, and non-denominational services. There is a "New Song" of adoration to Jesus, shared by millions.

"Shout to the Lord" has become one of today's best-known worship songs. Its writer, Darlene Zschech, likes to introduce herself as the mother of three and the wife of one, Mark. Darlene has been part of the Hillsong Church praise team since 1986 and has been leading the Worship and Creative Arts Department since 1996. As a worship leader, Darlene has to be a spiritual mom to those she trains and to the congregation as she leads them into the presence of God.

When I first met Darlene in the green room at the annual Worship Institute in Dallas, she looked straight into my eyes. A beautiful sixteen-year-old girl came and introduced herself as Sarah. Darlene immediately wrapped her arms around her and hugged her warmly. The young girl just melted and beamed, and I asked if this was her daughter. Darlene said that she had just met this darling girl today, as Sarah was helping host them at the conference. As I introduced myself and talked about the media schedule, Darlene kept her arm around Sarah until Sarah was called off to help run an errand.

Over the next few days I watched and listened as this "spiritual mum" of worship taught, modeled worship, and exhorted other worshippers to reach for new levels of holiness in God.

The Value of Building Up Others

When you watch Darlene interact with people, whether it is eating lunch or directing a choir of 300, she is constantly touching, nurturing, loving, affirming, encouraging, challenging, and pulling people into the presence of the Lord. She has a fire and passion for God that is warmth to the soul, and it spreads to others around her. Some people are God chasers—Darlene is a God walker. Darlene shares about the importance of being real in worship:

> Every time I worship I ask the Lord to touch my heart and change me. Giving God your heart and asking Him to change you has to be a willing decision on your part. If we don't ask God to change us then how can we expect others to enter in?
>
> As a worship leader I have to make sure that I am real and my relationship with God is real—real and not showy. I have to be connected so that I can help people to connect to the Father. Our team desires to lead people to the Lord and

get out of the way so that they can have a real encounter with the Lord.

Successful companies know how to protect their core values but remain flexible on the non-essential issues. At the Worship Institute, Darlene shared this example of how she has learned to protect the core values even when attack comes from within the team.

We had this very gifted individual who joined our team. And I began hearing that person asking questions about other team members and pastors that were slightly gossipy but nothing really serious. One day I overheard that person talking outside my office, and the conversation had shifted from "gossiping light" into murmuring. Immediately I asked the person to step into my office and explained, Honey, we don't do things like that around here. We don't talk about others in that manner. Later the person confessed that throughout their life this gossiping habit had caused problems and this was the first time it was confronted.

The enemy wants to sow seeds that will destroy the work of God. Seeds like gossip can eventually destroy the trust and relationships within your worship team and church. As a pastor and leader, you have to be diligent to recognize and deal with destructive behaviors immediately. It is critical to protect the core values so that God's work is protected.

Integrity Matters

Darlene believes that being a mother is one of God's greatest gifts, and she has learned to balance motherhood, ministry, and music by seeking God daily for His plan for the day. She knows that being grounded helps her keep the worship alive and fresh. True passion for God is developed not when you are in church but when you are alone with

God. Darlene tries to impart passion for God whenever or wherever she worships.

Darlene also believes in the importance of integrity. "The lack of integrity in a leader can undo in a day the work of a lifetime." She wants to equip the next generation to be radical Christ followers and to help them develop and increase their faith. "I want to see excellent worshippers inspiring the next generation to live wholeheartedly for the Lord. There are millions of young people begging for leadership that is radical in its commitment and true to its word. If your personal confession is full of negative words—a 'this is so hard' kind of vibe—or if your life is full of faithless stress, then your example will probably only repel those whom you have the opportunity to impact. Radical discipleship is needed!"

Spiritual Mothers in the Bible

Chapter Twelve

Elizabeth: A Spiritual Mom Trusted by God

*Blessed is she who believed, for there will be a fulfillment of
those things which were told her from the Lord.*
—Luke 1:45 NKJV

For with God nothing will be impossible.
—Luke 1:37 NKJV

Famous Mothers in the Bible for $500," shouts the game
show contestant.

"The answer is: Teen mom whose birth announcement
was delivered by angels," states the host.

"Who was Mary, mother of Jesus!" replies the winner
confidently.

When thinking of biblical mothers, Jesus' mother Mary
is the first response of most Christians. When thinking of
spiritual mothers, Elizabeth, the mother of John, is the first
example found in the New Testament. Elizabeth was a
woman who was trusted by God with more spiritual
responsibility than most people can imagine.

Elizabeth—Most Trusted Woman in the Bible

I believe that Elizabeth was the most trusted woman in the Bible for several reasons. First, as Scripture tells us, God trusted Elizabeth with being the mother of John the Baptist. Jesus called John the greatest man ever birthed to a woman (Luke 7:28). That is incredible praise. John the Baptist prepared the spiritual climate so that the Messiah could be received. I have known some remarkable mothers in my life, but Elizabeth must have been in a category all of her own.

Second, Elizabeth was the spiritual mom for Mary. When Mary was pregnant with Jesus, Elizabeth was the one who welcomed her, cared for her, fed her, blessed her, and shared the experience of pregnancy! She had less than three months to help prepare Mary for what was ahead of her. Elizabeth's faith, built by her own miraculous experience with God, must have strengthened Mary and helped her believe in her calling.

Finally, there is deep significance that Elizabeth was trusted above all other people with hosting and protecting Mary and her unborn child. This meant that the Lord trusted Elizabeth with the protection of His Son, the Living Word, during His first three months of life on earth. The first trimester of a pregnancy is the most difficult, and Mary needed more than a safe place to help protect the Son of God.

Now, let's glean more from the first example of spiritual mothering in the New Testament.

The Annunciation

I love the Book of Luke. I think of Luke as the follower of Christ most women would like to have over for dinner, because he is so good an including details in his stories. From this Gospel account, it is obvious that someone had spent time talking with Mary and other women to record the miraculous events surrounding Jesus' birth. These delicious details and human stories give wondrous glimpses into the lives of Mary, Joseph, Elizabeth, Zechariah, and others. These glimpses provide texture and emotion and help build our understanding of the remarkable events surrounding the Messiah's birth.

The angel Gabriel came to Mary and told her that she would give birth to the Son of God.

> *"How will this be," Mary asked the angel, "since I am a virgin?"*
>
> *The angel answered, "The Holy Spirit will come upon you, and the power of the Most High will overshadow you. So the holy one to be born will be called the Son of God. Even Elizabeth your relative is going to have a child in her old age, and she who was said to be barren is in her sixth month. For nothing is impossible with God."*
>
> *"I am the Lord's servant," Mary answered. "May it be to me as you have said." Then the angel left her.*
> —Luke 1:34–38 NIV

What an incredible encounter Mary had. As a young teen girl, how did Mary process this experience? How did she deal with the enormity of this announcement, and the stress of potential misunderstanding, rejection, or even death? Remember that in Mary's time, getting pregnant out of wedlock could mean that a girl and her child might be condemned to poverty, prostitution, or even death by stoning.

Mary was aware of these possibilities as she said, "May it be to me as you have said." Dealing with all these thoughts, fears, and options must have been difficult for Mary. But God in His wisdom and grace gave Mary a spiritual mom to help her make it through the difficult time. When Mary was told that Elizabeth was pregnant in her old age, she realized that there might be a person who would understand what she was going through. *"At that time Mary got ready and hurried to a town in the hill country of Judea, where she entered Zechariah's home and greeted Elizabeth"* (Luke 1:39–40 NIV).

It is clear that Mary didn't waste any time. She took action and immediately rushed to the home of her kinswoman, who had also experienced a miraculous pregnancy. As she made her way to the nearby hill country, Mary must have been nervous and apprehensive about arriving at the house of Zechariah and Elizabeth. How long had it been since they had seen each other? What would she say? How could she explain what the angel Gabriel had told her? Would Elizabeth be able to understand what this all meant?

We don't know if Mary would have heard about all the events, speculation, and gossip concerning Zechariah's angelic visitation and Elizabeth's miraculous pregnancy. We don't know if she knew that Elizabeth had been in seclusion for five months, never leaving her home or taking visitors. Mary might have wondered if Elizabeth would even see or speak to her. How difficult it must have been for Mary to carry this experience alone. She had to find someone older and wiser who would understand. Mary pushed through her swirling thoughts and fears to enter the courtyard of Elizabeth's home and greet her cousin.

When Elizabeth heard Mary's greeting, the baby leaped in her womb, and Elizabeth was filled with the Holy Spirit. In a loud voice she exclaimed: "Blessed are you among women, and blessed is the child you will bear! But why am I so favored, that the mother of my Lord should come to me? As soon as the sound of your greeting reached my ears, the baby in my womb leaped for joy. Blessed is she who has believed that what the Lord has said to her will be accomplished!"

—Luke 1:41–45 NIV

What a relief Mary must have felt when she heard Elizabeth's greeting and prophetic words! The Holy Spirit filled Elizabeth and confirmed all that Mary knew. How the weight of fears and self-doubts must have lifted. Joy must have flooded Mary's heart as she sang what is now known as the Magnificat, or Mary's Song:

My soul glorifies the Lord
   and my spirit rejoices in God my Savior,
for he has been mindful
   of the humble state of his servant.
From now on all generations will call me blessed,
   for the Mighty One has done great things for me—
   holy is his name.
His mercy extends to those who fear him
   from generation to generation.
—Luke 1: 46–50 NIV

How wonderful it was that Mary did not have to say a word to Elizabeth, because the Holy Spirit told her everything, instantly. God confirmed the truth of the angelic word with a prophetic word from Elizabeth. Immediately Mary knew that she was in the right place at the right time with the right people. The peace of knowing that she was in the center of God's will must have been incomparably joyous.

For the next three months, God covered Mary under the shadow of His wings. While she lived in the household of Zechariah and Elizabeth, Mary was hidden, loved, protected, and nurtured by this mighty woman of God, who became a spiritual mom to the mother of Jesus.

We know that Elizabeth was beyond childbearing years, which would have made her old enough to be Mary's mother, yet God in His great mercy gave them comfort in their fellowship. Being confined to a house with a husband who couldn't speak, for Zechariah had been struck dumb by the angel Gabriel, must have been lonely and difficult for Elizabeth. God gave Elizabeth a glorious distraction in the remaining months of her pregnancy.

Here's how I imagine it: Elizabeth taught Mary, and Mary helped Elizabeth physically. Like other women in stress, they did what they knew best; they talked while they tended to everyday needs. They ground grain, made bread, carried water, and talked. They sewed, they washed, they cooked, they cleaned, they ate, and they talked. This was a time to get everything ready for the sons of promise. These women were kept hidden but had the fellowship of each other to strengthen their faith. When women are pregnant, there is nothing more comforting than another pregnant woman to understand and share the experience.

How I would have loved to hear their conversations, their singing in the kitchen, their laughter at the birds, their joy at the rain. What did they talk about? What songs did they sing to the babies in their wombs? What dreams did they have? What prayers did they pray?

Like a colt on wobbly knees, Mary was fortified by Elizabeth until she could walk in paths of righteousness. Elizabeth knew that she needed to help strengthen Mary's spirit so she would not collapse under the criticism and rejection that would be waiting for her back in Galilee.

After three short months in the hills, Mary returned home fortified with the hope, faith, and love that Elizabeth helped build. Three months is not a long time, but the love between Mary and Elizabeth and the lessons that were learned were large enough to touch eternity's window.

Who was Elizabeth? Scriptures tell us (Luke 1:5–7) that she was a "daughter of Aaron," which means that she was from a priestly family. She was wife of Zechariah and kinswoman of Mary and was respected for her scrupulous obedience to all the laws, but was shamed by her childlessness. Barren until she was beyond childbearing years, this unlikely woman became the mother of John the Baptist.

How old was she? In pre-temple days, the average lifespan for women was thirty years, ten years less than the average for men, which was forty years. More than a third of a woman's life was spent in childbearing and tending children. Very few women lived beyond menopause, so Elizabeth and Anna (at the temple, Luke 2:36), were unusual. Elizabeth has been portrayed in movies as being in her late 40s or 50s, but she was probably much younger. She could have been as young as 30.

What's in a name? Elizabeth's name means "oath of God," but it has even greater meaning when you look at the root. Elizabeth is a version of the name Elisheba (el-ee-sheh-bah) that means, "my God has sworn" or "God is an oath," which is a stronger declaration of God's promises. Taking the name Elizabeth to the original roots, this name is a combination of *El*, which means God or God-like, (God's strength, power, and mighty things in nature) merged with *sheba*, which literally means seven. So the name Elizabeth promises that God's oath or covenant has the seven-fold strength of God.

Wives Carefully Chosen

Elizabeth was not your average woman; she came from priestly lineage and was given the same name of the wife of Aaron, the first priest and brother of Moses. The wives of priests were chosen very carefully, as they would have to lead and teach the younger women. When you consider all the laws and rules required for a traditional Jewish home, it is no wonder that girls required such training. As a priest's wife, Elizabeth would have been expected to keep an even higher standard than other women in her community.

The wife of a priest had leadership responsibilities within a community which would complement those of her husband. Just like the wife of a pastor or a commanding officer, the wife of the priest would be the person to whom women would come for counsel, training, and prayer. She would know when anyone was sick, pregnant, hungry, or in trouble. Elizabeth would have been the one to settle quarrels, call the midwife, and deal with the sick.

Leadership Lessons with Elizabeth

Living for several months with Elizabeth in a priestly household would have exposed Mary to both the administration and challenge of spiritual leadership. First, Elizabeth would have taught Mary how to keep the Jewish laws in a household like the priests did. Zechariah and Elizabeth were the spiritual leaders and models who taught the rest of the community, so Mary would have undoubtedly developed a new level of expertise by living with them.

Watching how Zechariah and Elizabeth interacted would have been a good example for Mary in her upcoming marriage. Not only would Mary have seen the spiritual devotion of a righteous couple, but also how this couple dealt with their own notoriety as the "miracle couple" in the spotlight of this small community. In fact, the lesson of "hiding things in her heart" until later may have been from Elizabeth's example of keeping her own counsel and going into seclusion at the beginning of her pregnancy.

Elizabeth's Spiritual Gifts

The prophet called out in the wilderness, "Prepare ye the way of the Lord." Yet before John even could speak, his mother was calling and proclaiming the presence of the Messiah. For decades, Elizabeth had been preparing her heart to teach the child that God had promised her. Elizabeth prepared the way of the Lord by offering her body to be used as a vessel to birth John, the forerunner of the Messiah. She prepared her home to receive the Messiah, carried in the womb of Mary, her spiritual daughter.

It makes you wonder: what it was like being around Elizabeth's faith? Did her eyes shine with the passion of knowing a secret that angels had whispered in her ears? What was her life like to have been trusted to be the hostess of the Son of the Lord God Almighty?

Elizabeth's devotion and love for God must have enhanced the spiritual gifts that she had been given. When she was filled with the Holy Spirit at Mary's arrival, Elizabeth was given the privilege to announce the arrival of the Messiah and bless Him in the womb. But Elizabeth did more than prophesy and welcome; she was the only person who was allowed to speak to Mary and Jesus for the critical first trimester. How incredible, to be the only person trusted by God to speak near His Son for the first three months of His life.

Was Elizabeth Rejected or Respected?

Strong spiritual gifts and godly visitations are not easy for the average person to handle. Elizabeth's gifts could have stirred up a great deal of envy and resentment from others. Being a person with a prophetic gift or special blessing from God is not easy. Prophets rarely win a popularity contest in the Bible or in life. They often get the "most likely to get stoned to death" award.

Based on the biblical account, it may be likely Elizabeth was not appreciated by those around her and experienced rejection in her community. Zechariah had to be silent as the miracle of John's birth played out. In Luke 1:20, Gabriel states that it was because of his lack of faith.

There is another part of the story that indicates that others did not accept Elizabeth for her spiritual understanding and opinion.

> On the eighth day they came to circumcise the child, and they were going to name him after his father Zechariah, but his mother spoke up and said, "No! He is to be called John." They said to her, "There is no one among your relatives who has that name." Then they made signs to his father, to find out what he would like to name the child. He asked for a writing tablet, and to everyone's astonishment he wrote, "His name is John."
> —Luke 1:59–63 NIV

With strong spiritual understanding and a prophetic tongue, Elizabeth must have been a threatening personality to some individuals. When they came to name the child, they argued with her and didn't listen to her when she said that the baby's name was John. John means "gift of God." What better name for this miracle child?

Once Zechariah told them that the child's name was John,

> Immediately his mouth was opened and his tongue was loosed, and he began to speak, praising God. The neighbors were all filled with awe, and throughout the hill country of Judea people were talking about all these things. Everyone who heard this wondered about it, asking, "What then is this child going to be?" For the Lord's hand was with him.
>
> His father Zechariah was filled with the Holy Spirit and prophesied.
> —Luke 1:64–67 NIV

Zechariah then declares a song of great beauty and strength over his son (Luke 1:67–79). The legacy that was to follow from John was to the credit of his parents.

Lessons from Elizabeth

So what do we learn from Elizabeth, spiritual mom to Mary? Mary may have been "Highly favored of the Lord," but Elizabeth was "Highly trusted of the Lord." Here are five key lessons from her life as a spiritual mom:

1. Elizabeth was a protector for Mary and for God's Son. Inspired by the Holy Spirit, Elizabeth confirmed what God was doing in Mary's life. Elizabeth helped to protect Mary and her child so that they had time to grow and be nourished. When God asks a person to do something really big, it is easy to have doubts. Doubts can turn into fears, and fears can paralyze and immobilize actions. Having another person tell us to "go for it" and that we really are hearing God's voice is extremely comforting. Spiritual moms help to protect the vision and dreams that God has for us, even when they only seem like tiny candles in caves of doubt.

2. Elizabeth spiritually fed Mary with food from both her physical and spiritual gardens. At Elizabeth's table, Mary probably was served fresh bread with daily portions of prayer, Scripture, and encouragement. Spiritual moms help teach us how to open our heart and ears to God. In their time together, Elizabeth taught Mary how to hear the voice of God more clearly, study the Scripture, and how to pray. Elizabeth understood that when you are in the desert of life, faith teaches you to dig deep wells of joy.

3. Elizabeth weeded the doubts from Mary's mind and heart. She taught her how to prune her doubts and send her thoughts in heavenly directions. Mary may have had questions like: "What do I tell my parents and Joseph?" "How will I deal with the shame and ridicule?" "If the officials find out, will they demand that I be stoned?" Undoubtedly, these concerns would have required days of conversation and prayer.

As Mary discussed these critical questions, she would have appreciated Elizabeth's wisdom and experience. One lesson that Elizabeth may have taught Mary was how to maintain peace in her heart and stand strong in the winds of doubt and unchanged by the clouds of confusion. There is a peaceful place in the center of God's will that Elizabeth could have helped Mary find and be anchored in.

4. Elizabeth would have also helped teach Mary how to lead. While she may not have needed these skills until later in her life, they were probably much needed during Jesus' ministry and in the beginning days of the church.

5. Elizabeth walked in faith and spoke in faith. When she said to Mary, "Blessed is she who has believed that what the Lord has said to her will be accomplished," she was speaking of herself as much as Mary. Elizabeth could teach this principle to Mary because she had lived it.

Scripture says that without faith it is impossible to please God. God showed His extraordinary pleasure and trust in Elizabeth by trusting her with the care, nurture, and protection of His Son. God showed that He trusted her life, voice, and love.

Faith is the assurance of things hoped for and conviction of things unseen. Elizabeth had the faith that allowed God to walk into her life and, through her, shape the future.

Chapter Thirteen

Huldah: Hidden But Not Forgotten

God Took a Nobody
God took a nobody to change a nation.
A person of no standing
to answer a King's question.
A nobody to reveal the truth.
A nobody with prophetic gifts to interpret a riddle.
A nobody was asked to declare the will of the Almighty.
A nobody spoke words that sparked national revival.
A nobody lit a fire that would burn
In the hearts of young men in Babylon.
A nobody was ready when the time came.
That nobody was Huldah.

When the king heard the words of the Book of the Law, he
tore his robes.
—2 Kings 22:11 NIV

God loves to use nobodies to shake foundations and light fires of revival. This is what happened in Judah, just prior to the Babylonian captivity. God used an unexpected discovery and an unusual alliance between a fiery young king and a wise spiritual mom to give the nation a spiritual "one-two punch" that would impact the entire world.

During the rule of young King Josiah, a scroll was discovered which contained the Book of the Law. The preceding kings of Judah had not been following the laws contained in the book for some time, and worship of other gods was widespread. The book pronounced disaster on Judah for all their idolatries. Josiah knew that the Lord's anger was great against them. Josiah had his priest and attendants go and inquire of the prophetess Huldah, who was the wife of the keeper of the wardrobe. Huldah had a word from the Lord for Josiah. Her words lit a fire under him that moved all of Judah to renew the covenant and walk in righteousness for the remainder of Josiah's reign (2 Kings 22–23, 2 Chronicles 34–35) The brief yet powerful words Huldah spoke instigated a huge movement to purify Israel, a movement led by Josiah.

Josiah—God's Fire for Judah

To understand how remarkable this is, let's explore what Scripture tells us about Josiah and his colorful family tree. Josiah's rule had a rocky start. Scripture says that both Josiah's father King Amon and his grandfather King Manasseh *"did evil in the sight of the Lord."* Both of them practiced idolatry and increased idol worship throughout Judah. (In 2 Chronicles 33, we read the story of Manasseh's repentance before the end of his life. He made attempts to rid the nation of idolatry, but his son Amon reinstituted the practices.) Two years after Amon took the throne, he was murdered by his advisers. Then, after Amon was murdered, Scripture says that *"the people of the land killed all who had plotted against King Amon, and they made Josiah his son king in his place"* (2 Kings 21:24 NIV). Josiah became King of Judah at the age of eight.

Thus Josiah, whose name means "fire of God," became king. Scripture says that from the time he was young he walked in the fear of the Lord (2 Kings 22:2). Josiah lit a fire for God that touched all of Judah. From the beginning of his reign, Josiah sought the Lord. He tore down Baal altars and purged the land of idols, Asherah poles, and false gods. In the eighteenth year of his reign, when he was twenty-six, Josiah began his efforts to purify the land and repair the Temple.

During this massive Temple project, the high priest found a Book of the Law. This scroll (probably a portion of Deuteronomy) had probably been hidden by the priests during the reign of the evil kings. To protect the scroll from destruction, it was probably wrapped and enclosed in a secret chamber by priests who were running for their lives. Josiah's reconstruction efforts lead to its discovery (2 Chronicles 34:14–18). When the scroll was read to the 26-year-old king, Josiah tore his robes in despair and sent his top advisors to the prophetess Huldah.

Huldah Who?

Huldah was the wife of Shallum, the keeper of the wardrobe. They lived in the Second District of Jerusalem, which in the King James Version is called the college (2 Chronicles 34:22). Huldah gave the king's advisors both bad news and good news. The bad news was that judgment was coming.

> This is what the LORD says: I am going to bring disaster on this place and its people, according to everything written in the book the king of Judah has read. Because they have forsaken me…and provoked me to anger by all the idols their hands have made.
> —2 Kings 22:16–17 NIV

Then Huldah gave them the good news: God honored Josiah's repentance and his prayers. Huldah told the king's men to take this message from the Lord to the king:

Because your heart was responsive and you humbled yourself before God when you heard what he spoke against this place and its people, and because you humbled yourself before me and tore your robes and wept in my presence, I have heard you, declares the LORD. Now I will gather you to your fathers, and you will be buried in peace. Your eyes will not see all the disaster I am going to bring on this place and on those who live here.
—2 Chronicles 34:27–28

The advisors took her words back to the king, and that is the last that we hear of Huldah the prophetess. There are several stories and theories about Huldah, such as that she was a teacher in the college, or that she taught the women around the Temple. A third story was that she tended the lamps around the Temple.

It is obvious that Huldah was a person of distinction; otherwise the king wouldn't have sent five of his top advisors to meet with her. Also, it is significant how Josiah responded to Huldah's words. God's words through her were unconditionally respected. The young king took immediate action and began a nationwide call to repentance. Josiah read the Book of the Law to all the people and renewed the covenant of Israel with God. Then, he instituted reforms, smashing and burning and sweeping out of Judah the idols, idolatrous priests, and symbols of idol worship, some of which had been installed in the Temple itself. He then celebrated a grand Passover that year, and Scripture says, *"none of the kings of Israel had ever celebrated such a Passover as did Josiah,"* (2 Chronicles 35:18). He provided sacrifices for the people out of his own flocks of sheep, goats, and cattle—more than 33,000 of them.

What Makes a King Righteous?
How does an eight-year old boy know what is righteous and how to live a godly life? If you were to look at Josiah's

heritage from his dad and grandfather, you would never have expected that he would become such a righteous king. To preserve his life you would have expected that there would have been a measure of religious activity, but Scripture tells us that from the time he was king, he sought the face of the Lord and walked in the ways of David.

With such a wicked father, where did Josiah learn to have such a pure faith? Who planted the seeds of truth and pruned his character? Who first lit the fire of faith in his life? Scripture does not tell us. Undoubtedly, with his father murdered, he would have cause to fear man, but his zeal for God demonstrates that his faith was genuine. One explanation is that Josiah could have received strong spiritual parenting and guidance as a child. It is possible that God surrounded this "young king of covenant" with a God-fearing mother or dynamic spiritual teachers who helped raise him up in the ways of God. Spiritual gifts are given to many, but without training even the most talented can fail.

A Trusted Nobody

A person's family helps us to better know what a person is like, and Huldah's family was short on position but high on trust. Huldah was the wife of Shallum, who was the keeper of the wardrobe of the kingly or priestly robes. That would probably mean Shallum was a staff member in a middle management position of responsibility like a butler or housekeeper for a royal family. Shallum was a trustworthy servant in this middle class position, but he would have had the honor of being close to the king or priests.

Shallum had a job of great responsibility and had earned this position through years of diligence and service. The royal and priestly garments were costly and difficult to make. They had cloth that was woven with gold and silver and sewn with jewels. These garments would have been locked in large trunks, and Shallum would have had a staff to guard, clean, and repair them.

In a world of machines and cheap textiles it is hard to imagine how much value a wardrobe had. Wardrobes were a display of position and a source of wealth. Textiles were a major industry of the day, as everything was made by hand. Garments were given as wedding presents, and young girls spent years sewing and preparing items for their household. Garments and embroidered scarves were given as spoils of war to the family of the warrior (Judges 5:30). In Nehemiah's time, the people of Jerusalem gave 97 priestly robes to the temple (Nehemiah 7:70–72). The robes of priests were considered holy, and a king's robes were treated with honor.

Even though Huldah's husband, Shallum, was only the keeper of the wardrobe, there is wonderful symbolism to his role. A robe represents a covering and authority. We can be dressed in the spiritual robes of God's righteousness or the filthy rags of our sin. Paul tells us to put on our spiritual armor and cover it with prayer (Ephesians 6:10–18). When we pray we cover others with God's blessings and protection.

Knock, Knock—Who's There?

Imagine being Huldah and having five of the king's advisors, including the high priest, show up at your door. This would be like having the vice president, Billy Graham, and three joint chiefs of staff knock on your door with a special message from the President. Talk about pressure!

Huldah was prepared when they showed up. First of all, Huldah knew that her job was simply to speak the word of the Lord, nothing more, nothing less. Four times she says, "This is what the LORD, the God of Israel, says." Huldah did not take credit or exalt herself. Huldah was a humble tool of God to declare truth and prophesy the coming disaster for Israel.

God used the humble woman to speak truth into the courts of the king. But what she was asked to do was be both a scholar of the Word and then prophesy what the Word of God was speaking to the nation. Why Huldah? Was it because she was trusted, faithful, above bribery and worldly influence? Was it because she taught at the Temple day in and day out? Was it because she knew the Word of the law and was ready when the moment of destiny came? Huldah was confident and had been around so long that she didn't care what people thought when she taught or spoke God's Word.

Ready to Touch the Future

We all have times in our lives when God wants to use us and our gifts through Him to touch heaven and birth new things into the Kingdom. Huldah was a spiritual mom to all of Judah. She was in the right place at the time because of her devotion to God. When God spoke through her, the king took action and the entire nation of Judah was touched by zeal for the Lord. Let's think for a moment about the impact of Huldah's words on the king.

God's prophetic word through Huldah did two things. First, it restored an intense spiritual devotion to Judah for more than a decade. It was a divine warning, mercifully given to Israel as their wake-up call. The second thing it did was to prepare the faith of the people before they went into exile. If their faith was to last through the seventy years of the Babylonian captivity, the children would have to be taught to be faithful.

When we look at the timeline we discover an interesting fact. The Book of the Law was rediscovered in 621

B.C., which began Josiah's reforms, and he died in 609. The first deportation to Babylon began in 605 B.C., four years after Josiah died. This means that all the adults, nobles, priests, worshippers, and servants had experienced Josiah's reforms and lived under them. As they were taken to Babylon, they would have understood the importance of Huldah's word and Josiah's call for repentance and renewal.

Fire Walkers

Four young men, Hananiah, Mishael, Azariah, and Daniel, who were in this first group taken into captivity in Babylon, were God's "fire walkers." (These are their Hebrew names; you might know them by their Babylonian names of Shadrach, Meshach, and Abednego.) The faith and dedication of these young men is legendary, as they resisted idolatry, obeyed the commandments, and survived the fiery furnace and the lions' den. These boys were born during the middle of Josiah's reform and grew up during it. It's plain from their story, found in the Book of Daniel, that these young men carried a pure, uncompromising faith in their hearts—a faith that was lit by the words of Huldah and fueled by the passion of Josiah. These young men carried into Babylon a faith that would touch the entire world and be strong enough to last seventy years and return again to Jerusalem. But that's another story.

The way God's Word moves through His people is always fascinating. God's Word traveled from the Temple where the priest found the Book of the Law to Josiah, from Josiah to Huldah, from Huldah to Josiah, and from Josiah to the people of Judah. It helped light the fires of faith that would burn in the hearts of the Babylonian captives.

What Do We Learn from Huldah and Josiah?

First, we learn that God uses people who are prepared to speak His words and change nations. He is not a respecter of persons, position, gender, or wealth. He is a respecter of hearts and actions. Huldah was a spiritual mom who was ready to be used by God and stayed humble in the process.

Secondly, we learn that God's timing is everything. It was no accident that the Book of the Law was found during the Temple reconstruction. When God is rebuilding things, hidden truths will appear and He will make His principles clear.

We learn to be courageous and speak the truth. Don't let the social position, financial status, or political power of others intimidate you or affect your spiritual abilities. Huldah knew who she was in God.

We learn to do our part. Huldah did her part to set things in motion and God did the rest. Your involvement in the plan of God may only require an hour, but it can change history. Do what God requires—no more, no less.

We learn the importance of teaching our children when they are young to walk in the ways of God, no matter what their family history is or what their relatives might have done. God will use children and young people to change the world, but they have to be taught.

And we learn that when you speak God's Word in the right season, it may ignite the fires of revival and touch millions or change the heart of a single young Daniel, whose faith lasted a lifetime and changed the hearts of kings.

Chapter Fourteen

Naomi: Unrecognized Spiritual Moms

I'd rather see a sermon
than hear one any day;
I'd rather one should walk with me
than merely tell the way.
The eye's a better pupil
and more willing than the ear,
Fine counsel is confusing,
but example's always clear...
For I might misunderstand you
and the high advice you give,
But there's no misunderstanding
how you act and how you live.
—Edgar A. Guest, *Sermons We See*

I was getting ready to make another cup of coffee as the phone rang. It was Janet, a friend who had moved to Oklahoma several months ago. As we chatted she shared how lonely she was in this remote area, miles from town and hours from any friends and family. She felt like her heart had been ripped when they moved, and it felt like she had a hole in her heart that was aching.

They had moved because her husband, Brian, formerly in the hotel business, had gotten a great business opportunity in northern Oklahoma. Janet and her husband had arrived at our church several years ago wounded, broken, and unsure of their faith. With time, prayer, and fellowship they were transformed into a beautiful young family who faithfully and elegantly catered any gathering or church event. It was hard for us to see them move and even harder for them to leave the area.

Janet's phone call to me was for encouragement and prayer. Without any hesitation, we prayed for strength and comfort for her in this "foreign land." We prayed that she would find new friends, fellowship, and a spiritual family where she would immediately feel at home. We asked the Lord to dispel this season of isolation with an even greater measure of His presence. We asked God to fill that hole in her heart with Him and that the bitterness would be changed into joy.

Mend and Tend

Moving away from family, friends, and fellowship is never an easy thing to do. This is especially difficult for women, who are natural relationship builders. In fact, women respond to stress much differently than do men.

A landmark UCLA study suggests that women respond to stress with a cascade of brain chemicals that cause us to make and maintain friendships with other women. Whereas men have the "fight or flight" response to stress and will tend to withdraw somewhere on their own, women have a "mend and tend" response and are calmed by tending children or gathering with other women.

Other studies show that the more friends a woman has, the healthier she is. This tendency to form friendships reduces the risk of disease by lowering blood pressure, heart rate, and cholesterol. Having friends helps women to live longer and to deal with stress.

Spiritual moms are often the first touch point for a person who is in crisis. When trouble hits, it is important that we have a safe place and find someone that we can talk to, someone who will not judge, someone who understands what we are going through—someone who has walked through the valleys and can show us the way out.

Scripture is filled with women who tended hearts and touched spirits, women who poured love into the lives of their biological and spiritual children and changed the world. One such person is Naomi, in the Book of Ruth.

Naomi: Hope for the Brokenhearted

Scripture always has such surprises for me. As I was choosing examples of women in the Bible who demonstrated the characteristics of a spiritual mom, I was amazed to discover how much Naomi's life and struggles touched me. When I was in my 20s, I studied Ruth's actions and had even memorized her "entreat me not to leave you" speech to deliver to a future husband. I hadn't really spent a great deal of time thinking about Naomi. In all the teachings, Naomi had been either ignored or judged very harshly for changing her name to "Bitter." But now that I have a little more life under my belt, many thoughts don't fit like they used to. I have a much more compassionate view of Naomi (and of many other people in the Bible.)

Studying Naomi's story, I recognized that many women today are struggling with challenges similar to Naomi's. Naomi had a very difficult life, filled with disappointment, sorrow, and struggle. She demonstrated faith and obedience even when dealing with basic survival issues, famine, widowhood, isolation, and living in an ungodly foreign land. And when she returned to her home village and her relatives let her down by not keeping the commandments of caring for widows, Naomi still responded with integrity and wisdom.

I believe that Naomi deserves credit for the spiritual mother she was and the impact her faith made. In our commentaries and teachings we have looked at the Book of Ruth through the "Cinderella Glasses" of our culture. These cultural glasses have a superficial view and have downplayed the hardships that built Naomi's character and the triumph over adversity that was then imparted to Ruth. The "Cinderella Glasses" tend to focus us on the romance and rescue aspects of the story and neglect the rich spiritual texture of the mother-daughter relationship. In short, the focus has been on Ruth, the beautiful heroine, and her romance with Boaz, rather than on exploring how Naomi helped Ruth, a Moabitess, became a woman who demonstrated godly principles worthy of being praised by the entire village.

Character Is Forged

Great character is not born; it is forged by fire and modeled during adversity. It has been my experience that character such as Ruth demonstrated doesn't happen by chance, but is taught, shaped, and developed by teachers and experiences that are placed in our lives. It is the character and faith of this older woman and unrecognized spiritual mom that provides the bedrock for the entire story.

Let me briefly summarize how the story of Ruth begins. (I would encourage you to take a few minutes and read the whole book. It is only four chapters, but it is a jewel of a story.)

There was a famine in Judah. Elimelech and his wife, Naomi, and their sons moved to the country of Moab. Elimelech died and left Naomi with her sons. Eventually the sons married Moabite women named Orpah and Ruth. After ten years, both of the sons died, leaving their young wives childless. Naomi heard that there was food once again in Israel and prepared to return, but told her daughters-in-law to return to their homes with her blessing that they would find new husbands. Both women were reluctant to leave. Finally Orpah agreed. But in one of the most moving declarations in scripture, Ruth pledged to stay with Naomi.

> *And Ruth said, Entreat me not to leave thee, or to return from following after thee: for whither thou goest, I will go; and where thou lodgest, I will lodge: thy people shall be my people, and thy God my God: where thou diest, will I die, and there will I be buried: the LORD do so to me, and more also, if aught but death part thee and me.*
> —Ruth 1:16–17 KJV

Naomi and Ruth returned to Bethlehem at the beginning of the barley harvest, and the entire town was stirred up because of their arrival. People didn't seem to recognize Naomi because of how different she looked. *"'Don't call me Naomi,'* she told them. *'Call me Mara, because the Almighty has made my life very bitter. I went away full, but the LORD has brought me back empty. Why call me Naomi? The LORD has afflicted me; the Almighty has brought misfortune upon me'"* (Ruth 1:20–21 NIV).

Most lessons about Naomi begin and end with this name change. Many times I have heard Naomi called an "old bitter woman," with the word *bitter* being linked to the New Testament Scripture in Hebrews 12:15, "See to it that no one missed the grace of God and that no bitter root grows up to cause trouble and defile many" (NIV). Bitterness and anger causes a breaking of covenant and relationships, both with God and with other people.

Was Naomi a bitter person whose heart turned away from God and poisoned the faith of others? Not according to the Scriptures. In fact, the declaration of Ruth's faith testifies the exact opposite of this. To claim that Naomi was filled with bitterness is not a correct interpretation. When Naomi used the word *Mara*, or bitter, she was describing the events of her life, not the condition of her character.

One reason is that the word *Mara* is a verb, not a noun. In those days, people would choose a name for children that described the events surrounding their birth, not their personality.

The name Naomi means "pleasant" or "my delight"— the opposite of her life experiences as a widow, childless and poverty-stricken. Imagine Naomi leaving Bethlehem, a beautiful young mother with a pleasant and outgoing personality. Then one day, twenty years later, an old woman with a young foreign woman arrives in the town. The old woman's face looks familiar, and when she tells her name, Naomi, people are stunned. First of all, imagine two women traveling alone in a time when thieves and bandits travel the few roads. These women must have looked terrible—dirty, starved, dehydrated, and exhausted. This unlikely pair's very presence and condition started everyone talking. *"When they arrived in Bethlehem, the whole town was stirred because of them, and the women exclaimed, 'Can this be Naomi?'"* (Ruth 1:19 NIV). "Can this be Naomi who left more than twenty years ago?" they must have said. "Her name is only a memory to us. What happened to her?"

In other words, there was a little shock factor when Naomi returned home. When Elimelech left with Naomi, the village probably assumed that this would be the last time that they ever saw them. In an agrarian society, farmers don't move once they get settled because it takes years to develop your land. Even today, how often do you hear about a farmer moving? You don't, unless they are bankrupt and their farm is foreclosed.

Tradition of Names

It is important to interpret Scripture by understanding both the core meaning of words and the traditions that shaped them. There are many things unsaid but assumed to be understood. For example, if I were to say, "Let's go to McDonalds," you would know that I meant a fast food restaurant instead of a friend's house, business, or city. In the naming process of children, we see that in biblical tradition, children are often named as a declaration of an event occurring at the time.

For example, Jabez means sorrow and seems to indicate that he was born in tragic circumstances, possibly the death of his mother. Yet when we discuss him we don't make character evaluations and call Jabez a sorrowful loser. In fact, because of the Jabez prayer, to our culture the name of Jabez is associated with blessing, success, and expansion.

So why did Naomi call herself "bitter"? Because Naomi was named "pleasant" and that is not what her life had been. When Naomi returned to her homeland, she was a woman in grief. If ever a woman deserved a grief recovery group, it was Naomi! How could she let herself be called "pleasant" when all she could do was mourn the loss of her husband and two sons, along with all her hopes and dreams? In times of grief, sometimes all people have is tears, so that is what they must bring to God.

Bitter Is Our Existence

There is great significance in the word that Naomi chose. *Mara* is the root word of the noun for "bitter herbs" that were to be eaten at the Passover meal. The bitter herbs and lettuces were to remind the Hebrews of the bitter bondage that they had suffered in Egypt. Bitter was the memory of the foreign land, but it is with joy they remember the salvation of the Lord.

In using the word bitter, Naomi gives several meanings to her return. She proclaims redemption from her bitter time of bondage in a foreign land. She is proclaiming that life was bitter away from Bethlehem and God's people. Mara, once Naomi, becomes a living declaration that when we live apart from the promises of God we can expect only the fruit of bitter disappointment and sorrows. As the exiled psalmist, removed from the Temple, grieves,

> By the rivers of Babylon we sat and wept when we remembered Zion....How can we sing the songs of the LORD in a foreign land? —Psalm 137:1, 4 NIV

Finally, the word *Mara* has an additional meaning of "to be strong or strengthen." Naomi was declaring that the bitter experiences had made her stronger than ever before. Spiritual moms know that while we cannot control our circumstances, we can allow them to make us stronger.

Did Ruth Think Naomi Was Bitter?

I don't think she did. You don't venture into the unknown with a person who is bitter. Bitterness of the spirit makes people sour to be around, and the negative attitudes make you want to run from them rather than cling to them. In a time of hardship and crisis, people do not take risks unless they are sure of something.

What Ruth saw in Naomi was enough to make her willing to forsake a predictable past for an unpredictable future. What did she see in Naomi? She saw a woman she wanted to be with and learn from. She had watched Naomi in the worst of situations, so she knew what to expect. This is a critically important point for leaders, mentors, and spiritual parents to remember. When you are in a leadership position, the people you are leading are watching to see how you react to every situation, both good and bad. How a leader responds will be watched and recreated by those around her. This is especially true for spiritual moms and dads; people are affected by what they see us do.

Ruth's Spiritual Heritage

Ruth's declaration of *"thy people shall be my people, and thy God my God"* explains that Ruth's faith was a serious spiritual commitment. This attitude is even more remarkable when you consider Ruth's spiritual heritage. The heritage of Moab was from the incestuous union of Lot and his daughter after the destruction of Sodom and Gomorrah. The name Moab means "Father, what father?" which explains the embarrassing heritage. Also, the Moabites were idol worshippers, considered unclean and not allowed into the Temple area. The reason for this is that when the Israelites wanted to pass through their land after the exodus, the Moabites were hostile and made the Jews circumvent their territory.

When you think about Naomi bringing two Moabite girls into her Hebrew household, she had a lot of work to do. In our terms, this would be the equivalent of having your Christian sons marry girls who were Buddhist or Hindu. The religious understanding and cultures are radically different. As Naomi believed that she would never return to Bethlehem, she had to carefully choose girls that could be converted into good Hebrew wives. Under the tutelage of their Hebrew mother-in-law, Ruth and Orpah would have been introduced to the Law of Israel, the commandments, the history, the customs, and the traditions. In a Hebrew household, Ruth and Orpah would have learned about Yahweh the living God. They would have learned about their identity and value as women. They would have heard about the matriarchal heroes like Sarah, Rebecca, Rachel, and Miriam.

When Ruth refuses to leave Naomi, saying "entreat me not to leave thee," I am reminded of the words of the disciples to Jesus: "Lord, where else can we go to find the words of eternal life?" Ruth may not have been raised in the Hebrew manner, but, through the life and spiritual mothering of Naomi, she had surely tasted the goodness of God and didn't want to return to her former culture. How could she return to that existence with its heritage of shame? Could she return to a family that would deny the truth of Yahweh and the hope that she found in Naomi? She had to go with her mother-in-law, and it was the truth of the "Ancient of Days" living in this spiritual mother that showed her that. It is said that the Lord's kindness leads us to repentance. In Ruth's case it was His kindness demonstrated in the faith and example of Naomi that provided the path to eternity.

Upon returning to Bethlehem, Ruth displayed character again and again through her obedience, self-sacrifice, hard work, and gratitude. All of these characteristics she had seen modeled in her mother-in-law, who was a true spiritual mother to her.

As we know, the rest of the story turns out well for Ruth and Naomi. Ruth proves her character and commitment through her tireless work and humility. She obeys all of Naomi's instructions and meets with continued success. Naomi's kinsman, Boaz, takes pity on the condition of these widows and gives protection and favor for Ruth's unselfish labor. Eventually Boaz becomes the true kinsman-redeemer for Ruth and Naomi and takes Ruth to be his bride. Ruth conceives and has a child, Obed, who is the father to Jesse, the father of King David, the ancestor of Jesus.

The Book of Ruth ends with such happiness and joy. When Ruth is married to Boaz, the entire city blessed the union and prayed that it would build the house of Israel. Their prayer was answered. Upon the birth of Obed, the women of the village came and proclaimed to Naomi:

> *"Praise be to the LORD, who this day has not left you without a kinsman-redeemer. May he become famous throughout Israel! He will renew your life and sustain you in your old age. For your daughter-in-law, who loves you and who is better to you than seven sons, has given him birth."*
>
> *Then Naomi took the child, laid him in her lap and cared for him.*
> —Ruth 4:14–16 NIV

How amazing! God honored the faithfulness of Naomi, Ruth, and the prayers of the people of Bethlehem. Naomi, once Mara, was restored. How the sweetness of this infant must have brought healing to Naomi. What indescribable joy and tenderness she must have felt. Naomi, who had sown in tears, was now reaping joy as she basked in the goodness of the Lord.

Chapter Fifteen

Deborah: A Leader for All Seasons

In the days of Jael,
The roads were abandoned;
travelers took to winding paths.
Village life in Israel ceased,
ceased until I, Deborah, arose,
Arose a mother in Israel.
—Judges 5: 6,7 NIV

In the early '80s I worked for a short period of time in Los Angeles. One of the jobs I had was working with a television producer helping him to develop treatments for made-for-TV movies and mini-series. Early in the process, I had the opportunity to practice "pitching" some of my movie ideas. Almost every plot line was shot down because the women in my stories were too strong. Several times, the studio executives and agents told me, "Give us victims!"

"The studios are only interested in TV movies that show the women as victims of a disaster, failed marriages, rape, financial struggles, loss of their kids," they said. "The viewers won't identify with strong women unless they are comedians. Make women victims so they will be believable and non-threatening to the housewives." Eventually, I gave up on movie business and went into the news industry where doors were flying open to hardworking women.

No wonder many women and girls don't believe they have value or can contribute to the world around them. The role models women are shown are feminine victims of life who survive the worst, find a Prince Charming to take care of everything, and live happily ever after. The plot lines are nothing more than slick romance novels that spin a web of seductive fantasy, make women objects of desire for men and deny their potential. The good news is that occasionally there are television shows and movies that break that mold.

However, sometimes the pendulum has swung too far in the other direction. Hollywood has gone to the other extreme and created a cast of bionic superwomen, that are projected as brilliant, kick-butt Barbie dolls with video-game attention spans.

It is great that Hollywood is developing movies and television shows with strong women who are smart enough to impact the world around them, but these superhero women are really nothing more than men in a feminine package. These characters negate the wonderful strength and power that a true woman of influence can have.

The Bible gives us an example of a woman who seemed superhuman in the story of Deborah, found in the book of Judges, chapters 4 and 5.

When it comes to leading, the best way is to work for or serve someone who is a great leader. Just like a doctor needs an intern program to practice with supervision, we need to have someone alongside when we are starting to walk in our spiritual gifts or career. In the time of Judges, Deborah's life casts an image through time that we need to learn from.

A Leader for Any Season

Deborah is one of my favorite women in the Bible. She was strong, wise and courageous. Deborah was the original "Woman Warrior." She was a visionary leader who did not shrink back from any command of God, even when others were fearful. Deborah led the nation of Israel from chaos into peace. When I think of women that are like Deborah, images of Joan of Arc, Margaret Thatcher, Indira Ghandi, Susan B. Anthony, and Harriet Tubman come to mind.

As a spiritual mother of Israel, Deborah led the entire nation through the seed, feed, weed and lead stages of growth. Her courage, vision and administrative ability restored God's blessings and order. We are in a season of history when God is calling forth the Deborahs, Baraks and Jaels to destroy the enemies that are within the gates of our cites and have entered our tents.

A Mother to Israel

This is what Deborah is called—a mother for Israel. Deborah was the first "titled spiritual mom" in the Bible. There were many mothers of the faith before her but she was the first in the Bible who was given the full job description.

Deborah's story is not a long one. This short account, rich in principles and imagery, is considered to be one of the oldest texts in the Bible. It contains a victory song composed by Deborah and the general Barak. For spiritual moms and all women today, Deborah's life is an inspirational blueprint for victory. This story reinforces the very promises of Eden and propels us with hope toward the book of Revelation.

Suggestion: Take a few minutes now and read this powerful story if you don't remember the full story. Read Deborah's song out loud and pay attention to whom she gives credit for the victory.

The story of Deborah is not a myth or fable. She was a hero and an important historical figure for Israel. Deborah was the third judge mentioned during the time of Israel's judges, and Deborah was special among them because she was a woman. She also carried a double portion of authority because she was a judge and also a prophetess. The only other one to carry this double role was Samuel.

The time between Exodus and the anointing of King Saul is called the time of Judges. For about 325 years, Israel was ruled by judges rather than monarchs. The nation cycled from obedience to disobedience and when they repented, God would give them a Judge to help deliver them from the cruel oppressor of the hour. In those days a judge was the voice of the law merged with political leadership. Deborah was number three in the Judges lineup.

Israel was in sad shape when Deborah emerged as a leader. Idolatry, danger, lawlessness, no commerce, no safety or national security—this is the situation Deborah stepped into. Her own words best describe what the true conditions were:

> The roads were abandoned;
> travelers took to winding paths.
> Village life in Israel ceased,
> ceased until I, Deborah, arose,
> Arose a mother in Israel.
> When they chose new gods,
> war came to the city gates,
> And not a shield or spear was seen
> among forty thousand in Israel.
> My heart is with Israel's princes,
> With the willing volunteers among the people.
> Praise the Lord!
> —Judges 5:6–7 NIV

We can tell that Israel was a weak, war-torn mess. Think Sarajevo, Iran, Chechnya, Afghanistan on their worst days. A place where the bad guys rule and the good guys pay for protection—a nation that lives in fear and where mothers can't let their children play outside. A country where people don't even have a sword, spear, arrow to defend themselves from attack. Conquering kings would gather up all metal implements and reforge them into weapons for their own armies, and the people lost their tools for harvesting.

Israel was a country in chaos, in need of a visionary leader with strong administrative skills and eye for talent. A leader who would be willing to make the sacrifice to turn things around. Who did they call upon? Judge Deborah.

Deborah's name means sacrifice, or to offer a sacrifice, as in animal sacrifice. Judge Deborah was the one who sacrificed herself to bring Israel back into order. She loved the princes and the common people of Israel. As the judge, she restored God's law and obedience to it, which helped to restore God's blessing to His people. This wasn't an overnight process. It took years for Deborah to purge idolatry and lawlessness from the nation. But when she did, life was restored and communities began to thrive. Her courage helped to strengthen the people of Israel so that they were able to eventually overthrow their oppressors and have peace for forty years.

At the height of her office, the Lord spoke through Deborah and commanded Barak to gather troops to destroy Sisera, who was the commander of Jabin's army. Jabin was the Canaanite king who had been oppressing Israel. This was no easy request because Sisera had a huge war machine of nine hundred chariots, and Israel was struggling to simply find swords. This would be like telling a group of Marines with handguns to take out a battalion of tanks. Without God's intervention in a task like this, it would be impossible. Barak was naturally hesitant.

In simple Hebrew, Barak tells Deborah, "Okay, if you are this confident in this word, then you come with me to battle."

"Very well," Deborah said, "I will go with you. But because of the way you are going about this, the honor will not be yours, for the Lord will hand Sisera over to a woman" (Judges 4:9a NIV). Barak gathers ten thousand men and they go to meet Sisera with nine hundred chariots by the Kishon River.

The Battle

What happened can only be explained as the miraculous hand of God. Edith Deen, in her book *All the Women of the Bible*, explains:

> We learn from Josephus and indirectly from the song of Deborah that a storm of sleet and hail burst over the plain from the east, driving right into the face of Sisera and his men and charioteers. The slingers and archers were disabled by the beating rain, and the swordsmen were crippled by the biting cold.
>
> Deborah and Barak and their forces had the storm behind them and were not crippled by it. As they saw the storm lash the enemy, they pushed on, believing all the more in providential aid. The floodwaters were now racing down the Kishon River. So violent was the rain that Sisera's heavy iron chariots sank deep in the mud and as they did, many of the charioteers were slain. And the hoofs of the cavalry horses splashed through the mud as a small remnant made its retreat.

Sisera abandoned his army and fled on foot to what he believed would be a safe location, the tent of Jael, wife of

Heber the Kenite. Even though the Kenites were longtime allies of Israel, Heber had thrown in with Jabin and his forces. In spite of social taboos, Jael greeted Sisera, hid him in her tent, and gave him milk to drink. Sisera lay down to rest. While Sisera was fast asleep, Jael took a tent peg and drove it through his head. When Barak arrived he found Sisera dead and the honor for the battle was given to Jael, a dweller in tents. It was that day that the Israelites subdued Jabin and eventually they got stronger until they destroyed him.

Most Blessed of Women?

The victory over Sisera and Jabin was a great mark for Israel. But in truth, I've always felt a bit squeamish about what Jael did to Sisera. To put a spike through the head of an ally is not on Emily Post's list of "How to deal with unexpected houseguests." Yet Deborah calls Jael the most blessed of women, of tent-dwelling women (Judges 5:24). How could a murderer be the most blessed of women? And why did Jael go against Sisera, with whom her husband had "friendly relations" (Judges 4:17)?

There could be several reasons. First, by killing Sisera, Jael was honoring the older alliance with Israel that superceded her husband's relationship with the Canaanites. Jael could have had Hebrew roots or followed the faith of the God of Abraham, Jacob, and Isaac. Or Jael could have had a friendship with Deborah that was stronger than Heber's temporary alliance with Jabin.

What we do know is that Deborah and Barak put Sisera on the run, and he ended up at Jael's tent. Deborah's role as a spiritual mother of Israel helped launch and empowered Jael's action, which secured Israel's victory.

Back to the Garden

Jael's action is a fulfillment of one of the most important promises that a woman ever received. Back in the Garden of Eden, when God passed judgment on the serpent, woman is given a promise:

> *And I will put enmity between you and the woman,*
> *And between your offspring and hers;*
> *He will crush your (serpent's) head, and you will strike his heel.*
> —Genesis 3:15 NIV

God promises woman that her offspring will crush the head of the enemy. The King James Version uses the word bruise instead of crush, but in reviewing the Hebrew roots, crush is a better translation. The Lord promises that the seed of woman would crush, shake from a high place, and annihilate the head and rule of the enemy. The serpent and his seed were to strike at the heel of man. The heel relates to a person's walk. The word "strike" means to trip up, supplant, and seize or restrain (as if holding by the heel). The promise of this verse is that God, through Christ, gives us authority to crush the enemy's rule over our lives. The enemy may try to trip us but when we walk the path of obedience and stay in the will of God we are protected by His grace. We are seated in high places with Christ.

Jael was "most blessed of women" because she was able to fulfill the promise of victory that God gave in the Garden of Eden. When Sisera was defeated in battle, he tried to hide in the tent of a woman. When Sisera, the enemy, tried to hide in her tent, Jael took the only weapon she had, a wooden nail and hammer to kill him. The symbolism of this is so rich. First Sisera (even his name sounds like a snake!) was killed. Sisera was in Jael's tent, which was forbidden, so she had dominion over her home. The wooden peg is representative of the wooden cross and nails of the crucifixion. Jael took the authority of the cross and destroyed the intruder who had entered her tent, her life, and her destiny.

Jael represents what every person is called to do when the enemy is in our tent, homes, business, and relationships. We are to take the promises of God and the victory of the cross and use them to destroy every thought, behavior, attack that comes against Christ. We must depend upon the power of the cross to put down and subdue everything that is against God's purposes for our lives, and those of our family, church, businesses, and world.

In simple terms, we use the seeds of our words, prayers, worship, praise, actions and service to establish the truth and peace of God in our life. "Take up the Cross" has whole new meaning, not for suffering but for victory—its promises, the blood, the mystery, the grace and the strength—causes us to proclaim, "The Wondrous Cross!"

> When I survey the wondrous cross,
> On which the Prince of glory died,
> My greatest gain I count but loss
> And pour contempt on all my pride.
>
> See from his head, his hands, his feet,
> Sorrow and love flow mingled down
> Did e'er such love and sorrow meet
> Or thorns compose so rich a crown?
>
> Were the whole realm of nature mine
> That were a present far to small
> Love so amazing so divine
> Demands my soul, my life, my all.
>
> —Isaac Watts

Conclusion

Spiritual Moms with Global Compassion

*A spiritual mom
is like a
diamond,
dancing in the sunlight,
whose brilliant facets
are uncountable.*

I have twin nieces, Claudia and Laura, who are truly delightful seven-year-olds. While visiting their house, I was given the royal tour of their bedroom. This was not a normal tour. I anticipated that there would be dozens of creatures, but I was not prepared for a trip to the "Animal Metropolis."

There were three complete dollhouses with multiple families, animals, and offspring. Along the wall were cardboard houses, each with their own family, history, and function. The girls had named literally hundreds of stuffed and plastic animals, Beanie Babies, and Happy Meal toys. They had created family histories, built relationships, and woven epic stories for even the smallest of the toys. Each creature had an identity and was connected in community. I was astonished with the complexity of details and their ability to remember everything.

In the room, there was even a bench that was the hospital waiting room. The girls carefully explained which of the animals were ill and which of the remaining dozen were pregnant. They like to call these prolific creatures breed-a-holics.

Later their mom, Susan, told me that the girls wanted to make sure that I had gotten the right impression of who they were. They had decided, because I was the "working aunt," that they needed to make sure that I didn't think they were too girly and liked dolls too much. They had purposefully put away all the Barbie dolls before I arrived because they wanted me to know that they were more mature than other seven-year-old girls. They wanted me to know that they liked animals better than dolls.

Now the twins didn't need to worry about me thinking they were too girly because of a few Barbies. One short visit to their "Animal Metropolis" was all that was needed to taste how strongly, even at seven years old, the twins were able to demonstrate the wonderful female gifts of nurturing and building community. This visit gave me a glimpse of what incredible young women Laura and Claudia will be as they grow into their destinies in the Lord.

Women Are Life Weavers

Before I formed thee in the belly I knew thee; and before thou camest forth out of the womb I sanctified thee, and I ordained thee a prophet unto the nations.
—Jeremiah 1:5 KJV

While we were in the womb, God was knitting all of our parts together. As the "womb" of the family, women also knit the family together. Maybe this is why knitting and weaving come so easily to women. It is a physical manifestation of the natural gifts God gave women. Women tend to be the ones who are linking people's lives together with meals, activities, and memories. Women are "life weavers."

Women are also crafters. Scripture says that man was formed from the dirt but women were crafted from the rib of man. Women were crafted, and they in like fashion craft everything around them. Women decorate themselves and the home, gather elements for cooking, and create thousands of gifts for others. God uses women to craft and create beauty as well as weave the lives around them into the complex and incredibly beautiful elements of community.

A Famous Mother's Challenge

When the main speaker was introduced at the Presidential Prayer Breakfast in Washington, D.C., the entire room strained to see. A wheelchair was rolled onto the platform and Mother Teresa waved gently with one hand and clutched her notes with the other. As she came into view, the entire room stood and applauded; many of the dignitaries were shouting. This was unusual for the Washington culture, which is normally very restrained and polite. Such emotion is only displayed at winning football games or inaugural parties.

It was extraordinary, but when Mother Teresa entered, from the back of the room we could feel a wave of warmth flood across the room. There was something about the presence of this frail, white-robed woman that invoked respect and awe. As I looked around the room filled with senators, congresspersons, ambassadors, business leaders, and dignitaries, many eyes were brimming with tears.

Mother Teresa's presence at the breakfast was a surprise because she had been weakened by a heart attack. As they helped her up from the wheelchair, it was obvious how weak she was physically. When she stood at the podium, all you could see was the white cloth covering the top part of her head. She was so little to have such a mighty presence.

She held her notes and began reading with a heavily accented voice. Even though it was difficult to understand all of the words, there was no doubt of the strength of conviction that her voice projected.

Her message was based on Matthew 25:40: *"I tell you the truth, whatever you did for one of the least of these brothers of mine, you did for me"* (NIV). The core of Mother Teresa's speech was that the greatness and character of a country and its people is measured not by its wealth or power but by how they treat "the least of these"—those who cannot take care of themselves.

Mother Teresa then challenged us all to rise up and embrace the divine call to bring the love of Jesus to all. The world and heaven watch and weigh our value by how we treat the old, the young, the infirm, and the handicapped. As she spoke, the President kept his eyes fixed on Mother Teresa and didn't move a muscle.

When a spiritual mother speaks, even presidents listen. A spiritual mom can say things to leaders that no one else can. On an international basis, spiritual moms are coming into a new place of prominence in the world. Spiritual moms are hearing the cries of the widow, the orphan, the poor, the diseased, and the lost and finding ways to help.

Spiritual Mom with a Global Reach

There are many spiritual moms around the world who are heroically addressing these issues. Winnie Bartel is one of those women. To meet Winnie you would never know that this farmer's daughter, wife of a farmer, and grandmother is helping to unite women across international, racial, denominational, and political boundaries. She and many other women are weaving a glorious net of relationships, which are helping to spearhead social, economic, and religious reforms across the globe.

Winnie Bartel is the executive chair of the World Evangelical Fellowship's Commission on Women's Concerns. In 2001, she was also the chair for the Global Celebration for Women, which was a historic gathering of Christian women leaders from over 160 nations. The event happened the week after the terrorist attacks of 9/11. Because Winnie and thousands of others have been willing to sacrifice their personal agendas and unite, people are being mobilized and lives are being rescued from abuse, poverty, and disease. Winnie shares, "The bottom line is to mobilize churches, so we are calling leaders together. Women leaders gather to share, pray, encourage one another. Then we decide which issues to address and mobilize for action, start programs, and partner with ministries to help meet the needs of families, churches, and society."

One of the first issues that Winnie and the leaders addressed was the rising rate of physical and sexual abuse of women worldwide. A study and book were published, *No Place for Abuse: Biblical and Practical Resources to Counteract Domestic Violence,* by Catherine Clark Kroeger and Nancy Nason-Clark. For more information about Global Celebration for women go to www.globalchristian-women.org.

Desert Blessings

Spiritual moms know that God is faithful even when He leads us into the desert and wilderness. The desert season ignites a bonfire from heaven within that helps to light the way to our greatest victories.

When we take action to do something that God has called us to do, we often aren't quite sure if we've got it all right. That is why it is called a faith walk instead of a "know-it-all journey." The more we grow in God, the more confident we become in His goodness and have fewer ropes to hold on to. Missionaries inspire us because when a person works in a foreign culture, faith is often the only assurance that one can bank on.

My friend Jack worked in war-torn Sudan during the early '90s. They smuggled Bibles and literature into various parts of the country and had to deal with extreme danger, heat, and hostile governments. Sudan is a country about the size of Texas and only has very few drivable roads. To reach remote locations across the sub-Sahara plains, they would navigate with a compass, map, stars, and prayer. They would drive for several nights and sleep under the trucks during the day when the heat reached temperatures well over a hundred.

One early morning, after driving across the desert all night, Jack was hopeful that they were nearing the village they had aimed for. As they drove over a final dune, they saw in the distance a hill with an old man waving to them. They drove cautiously toward him, not knowing what his intentions were. As they pulled up, the old man looked happy to see them, and Jack and his guys took a deep breath. They asked for directions to the village and the old man pointed to a location a short distance away. Jack explained that they had books and things to sell to the villagers. (It was against the Muslim law for them to distribute Bibles, but they could "sell" material.)

The village father looked at Jack with wrinkled eyes and he asked him a very direct question. "What took you so long?"

Jack was a bit taken aback because in this culture it is socially unacceptable to ask direct personal questions unless you are looking for trouble. Jack answered, "Excuse me, father, do we know you?"

The old man took a deep breath. "No, but I knew that you were coming."

"How, father, who told you?"

"No one told me." The look again pierced Jack's soul as if to weigh it and see if it was worthy.

The old man continued with measured words, "I had a dream. I had been praying and asked God to give me truth. And in my dream He told me that white men with beards would come across the desert in the morning and give me a book of life. This book would tell me the truth. You are the men that I saw in my dream."

Jack and his team breathed a sigh of relief and joy. Jack immediately went and got a Bible for the old man, one that had been translated into his language. They started to get back in the truck, grateful that God had faithfully guided them across the desert to this precious grandfather. Thinking that the old man had been waiting for them through the night, Jack asked, "Father, how long have you been waiting?"

"Twenty years. For twenty years I have come every morning to the top of this ridge to look for you and make sure that you could find your way to our village." The old man closed his mouth and nodded his head up and down with conviction as his eyes filled with emotion. Jack couldn't see the rest because he was weeping.

****

Like the old man on the hill, people—old, young, rich, poor, strong, and weak—are waiting for someone to reach across the desert of their lives to bring them the words of life. There are many valleys and deserts that people have to cross. Spiritual moms are like streams in the desert and so much more.

What Is a Spiritual Mom?

She is like the diamond dancing in the sun, whose brilliant facets are uncountable. Spiritual moms are able to able to touch heaven with prayers for those they love. They are seed carriers for God, and nobodies who are called to speak the truth. They are trusted like Elizabeth and Huldah. They are steadfast like Naomi. They have walked through valleys of sorrow, yet are covered with a beautiful strength that radiates from them. They nurture the growth of faith.

Spiritual moms are world changers. Some change the world around them and others change the world inside us. There are so many women, known and unknown, who have touched the world—so many heroes that we need to be proud of, so many who have touched heaven on our behalf.

Spiritual moms are warriors in the spirit and fighters for God's Word. These women are writing a new testament to the work of God in our time. They are living testimonies that will defeat the enemy—testimonies that reflect the light of Christ and are filled with power.

Spiritual moms are blessings multiplied—
   Gifts from God,
   Songs of truth in times of doubt,
   Beacons of light in life's darkest storms,
   Hugs filled with love in the coldest season,
   Touches from heaven in a foreign land.

Spiritual moms are heroes of the heart because spiritual moms come from the heart of the Father.